THOSE
FIRST
AFFECTIONS

Dancing, by Clare Brett age 5

THOSE
FIRST
AFFECTIONS

AN ANTHOLOGY OF POEMS
COMPOSED BETWEEN THE AGES
OF TWO AND EIGHT

Collected and introduced by

TIMOTHY ROGERS

With a foreword by

CHARLES CAUSLEY

ROUTLEDGE & KEGAN PAUL
London, Boston and Henley

First published in 1979
by Routledge & Kegan Paul Ltd
39 Store Street, London WC1E 7DD,
Broadway House, Newtown Road,
Henley-on-Thames, Oxon RG9 1EN and
9 Park Street, Boston, Mass. 02108, USA
Set in Baskerville 11/12pt by Columns
and printed in Great Britain by
Lowe & Brydone Ltd

British Library Cataloguing in Publication Data

Those first affections

1. Children's writings, English
2. English poetry — 20th century
I. Title
II. Rogers, Timothy
821'.9'1408   PR1178.C5   79-40658

ISBN 0 7100 0303 X
ISBN 0 7100 0304 8 Pbk

For Jennifer, Jonathan and Nicola,
who would not otherwise appear

A Duck, by Magnus Gregory age 5

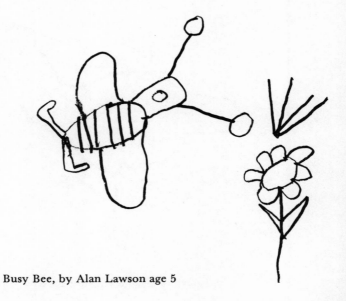

Busy Bee, by Alan Lawson age 5

CONTENTS

Those first affections,
Those shadowy recollections,
Which, be they what they may,
Are yet the fountain light of all our day
Are yet the master light of all our seeing.
William Wordsworth

FOREWORD

'Now, what I want is, Facts. . . . Facts alone are wanted in life,' declared that 'eminently practical man' Mr Gradgrind of Coketown in *Hard Times*. Dickens's novel was published in 1854, but it would be useless to deny that the baleful shadow of Thomas Gradgrind does not occasionally still fall across the path of the young, whether at school or in the home.

It is, however, a shadow slowly fading. A century ago, the main object of education was generally accepted to be the cultivation of human intelligence. One of the most significant developments in educational thought today is the belief that the cultivation of the creative imagination is at least of equal importance, if not more so. A suspicion has grown into a certainty that the provision of facts, for themselves alone, is simply not enough. Time and bitter experience have bred a healthy distrust.

Why should this be so? One of the finest of the present generation of poets, Ted Hughes, effectively answered the question when he said, 'The objective, scientific, fact watching attitude, and [the] detached, passively recording attitude, is of no use whatsoever when it comes to dealing with our own minds and hearts. It is useless in the most vital activity of all. The activity of understanding ourselves.'*

One of the processes that first sets this activity in motion, albeit unconsciously, is the deep need of a child to 'taste' and familiarize himself with language; to explore it inventively; to orient himself, like a creature emerging from a world of semi-darkness, in a dazzling, new-found map of speech.

A child's first verse, invariably, is the equivalent of a cry of joy: a rhythmic and rhyming couplet that eases the stiffness of the tongue and releases the spirit. It is the voicing of a spell or charm by means of which the speaker may relate, with increasing confidence, to his surroundings. It may also, at this stage, more closely echo music than resolve itself into the rationale of ordered speech. The sound, here, may be pre-eminent. The sense — and with it, the poem — is to follow as mind and imagination cohere and develop.

* *Children's Literature in Education.*

FOREWORD

A poem must possess qualities both of mystery and revelation. It may tell us something of its subject, its author, of the world, and — by a mysterious process of reciprocal communication — something of ourselves. The fact that the poems in the collection that follows happen to have been written by children is, in a certain sense, irrelevant. A poem is a poem. We should beware of a patronizing attitude. To treat the anthology merely as a collection of literary curiosities, as a succession of clever and amusing performing tricks with words, would be to miss the point. The vision may sometimes seem strange, bizarre, perhaps even (in the best sense of that much-misused word) shocking. But such properties should be recognized, and welcomed, as both fitting and salutary. However daunting and difficult a form of expression the work of a child may take, it is absolutely necessary that we should try and comprehend it; that we should genuinely seek to understand just what factors, just what secret or half-concealed elements, may have contributed to its making. A child has produced what is evidently to him or her a clear, creative statement. The rest, quite naturally, is up to us.

At the same time, I feel it a permanent necessity (particularly if one is working as a teacher in the field of what, in a slightly unhappy phrase, is known as 'creative writing') to maintain a proper sense of balance. It would be just as undesirable to treat the original poetry of children with excessive weightiness and solemnity as it would be to ignore or undervalue its rare revelatory qualities.

The 'adult' poet, particularly when writing for an audience he knows will be composed mainly of children, needs to remain resolutely aware of the fact — again — that a poem is a poem, or nothing. On the subject of verse written by adults for children, W.H. Auden remarked tellingly, 'While there are some good poems which are only for adults, because they pre-suppose adult experience in their readers, there are no good poems which are only for children.'* There should, then, be no hint of 'writing-down'; no dilution of poetic spirit. Nevertheless, communication (though not necessarily instant communication) is all, or nearly all. But who dares to say, with confidence, that he understands *everything* in a poem? The lesson of poetry is that at the heart of the

A Choice of de la Mare's Verse (Faber, 1963).

x

simplest-seeming work is an area unfathomed and unfathom-able. It is the unseen source of existence that yields the con-tinued life of a work in art, and to the creation of which every artist instinctively directs himself.

All art demands, at very least, respect. Certainly, when considering the work of children, it requires the same respect and seriousness from the adult as that with which a child invariably himself approaches the task of creation. There should be no boundary lines between adult and child, or creator and creator. And of one thing we may be perfectly certain: that the writing of poetry cannot be taught. The impulse to attempt its making may, rather, be caught by attrition from the enthusiasm and commitment of another. But it must be a genuine enthusiasm, a true commitment: never an attitude adopted (even with the best of intent) for the purposes of 'instruction' or 'education'. The instinct of imaginative creation, once stimulated in a child, is a key to joy. Too often it is not realized (and this, particularly so, among young children) that creativity in art is not of neces-sity related to intellectual power, to 'brains', and to more easily defined and calculable abilities. The sources of creativ-ity are more mysterious. Pleasantly enough, they defy the normal processes of measurement and assessment, and remain quite unrelated to known scales of 'intelligence'.

It is too often assumed that a child fluent of speech, apparently well-gifted in written skills, will be equally skilled and effective in the quality of his original, creative writing. But, in my experience, I have found this to be by no means the general case. Indeed, an awful fluency, in which the pen barely marks the surface of the innermost feelings and thoughts of the writer, may initially be a grave source of difficulty; may produce little but barely considered exper-ience, observation, emotion. A struggle, on the other hand, through the thickets of inarticulacy, may often produce work of real depth and quality.

In reading and assessing the work of children, a fearful responsibility rests with the adult reader. Sadly, I feel, a great deal of excellent writing goes unremarked. By the nature of things, also, a good general teacher cannot be expected to be expert in the assessment of original verse. But the Russian poet and writer Kornei Chukovsky, in his brilliant study *From Two to Five*,* points clearly towards what might be the best contribution from the teacher in the delicate processes of original composition.

> When the children sing, clap, play, or work out a project, I look on with the greatest pleasure. When they begin to read me poems that have been taught to them in school ... I often feel like a real martyr. Together with the work of our classical poets, they have been taught hackneyed lines, absurd rhythms, cheap rhymes. There are times when I could cry with disappointment. I am convinced that exposing children to such trash will cripple their aesthetic tastes, disfigure their literary training, and condition them to a slovenly attitude to the written word, and that all this rubbish will block off the children's appreciation of genuine poetic works. However, my author's grief was incomprehensible to some of the educators, as these excellent people (so useful in other ways) had been deprived of literary culture. They had no criteria for evaluating works of poetry.
>
> In almost every kindergarten and every child centre, in every school, I met promising children, who, under different circumstances, could be developed into good writers; but their giftedness withered in the nonliterary environment in which they found themselves. The 'corrections' made in their verses by the teachers were almost invariably worse than the original version.

The warning is clear; and if it is true — as I believe it to be — that in their writing, children may reveal unparalleled glimpses of the lost world of childhood, as well as an often devastating view of our own present, then we dare not disregard such an opportunity of re-assessing, re-valuing those worlds in order that we may better understand our children and ourselves. For the child possesses, by nature, that valuable quality all adult artists seek to retain, or regain: the ability of being able to view the world, seen and unseen, *as if for the first time.* The true vision of the child is unblurred by time and experience, tact and expediency; a picture of themselves, and of us, apt to be informed with a

* University of California Press, 1971.

disquieting simplicity and strength and candour.

A very great deal of poetry, in the final count, is also autobiography. This is especially true of verse written by children. What, on the surface, might appear to be the most extravagant flight of fancy is frequently to be seen as the direct result of a necessity — invariably quite unconscious — of the child (and poet) to create those myths he most needs to help him understand something of the mystery of life.

The value of a collection as carefully chosen as that which follows is many-sided. Not least, I think, is that it may help those involved with creative writing among children to establish some kind of touchstone, some kind of reliable standard, against which original work written by others might be measured. Given sympathetic encouragement, the right environment, the necessary stimulus, and an abundant supply of patience among all concerned (for art will not be hurried), it would seem to me that results elsewhere are likely to be at least as high; perhaps, one is bound to hope for art's sake, even higher. The creative spirit, very properly, knows no bounds.

Given absolutely none of these stimuli, the good poem, as all teachers and parents well know, still has an encouraging habit of emerging; and, lest we strive for conditions too sweet and comfortable in the making, we must always needs remember that art is also the product of tension and the result of an attempt to resolve the effects of opposing forces.

The practice of encouraging creative writing among the young (or, indeed, any age-group) is, nevertheless, not primarily a literary one. There is no intent to produce a nation composed entirely of poets and novelists, playwrights and short-story writers. Generally, the 'born' writer, somehow, will make his way; his nature is such that, as often as not, he has no choice. But I have never felt the writing of verse (or creativity in any art-form) to be the prerogative of a small *élite*, of a particularly and peculiarly gifted group within a society. I hold, rather, that it is something to be practised with perfect validity and, within its own terms of reference, with every possibility of real success, by all who, at certain moments in life, feel the need, indeed the necessity, of doing so.

The principal aim of the poet in writing poetry is not

necessarily publication; neither is that of the painter, for instance, to get his work into an art-gallery. Publication, exhibition, may be pleasant concomitants of the act. But its central importance, as a human activity, and its real value, whether to adult or child, must always lie in the *doing*. It is a self-realizing, life-enhancing sphere of action: and its habitation is a country of the mind and the imagination to which everyone, from earliest childhood, should be conscious of the free and unencumbered right of access.

CHARLES CAUSLEY

INTRODUCTION

'I wonder how God got it in his heart to make the sea?' In these words a young child expressed his excitement at a first glimpse of the sea. Another child, who was older, and who had been intrigued to hear of blank verse and how it should have five feet with two beats in each foot, wrote this: 'One day/ Posei/don grown/ strong will/ conquer.' The second child was Rupert Brooke, then aged about ten, and the carefully wrought pentameter was from his earliest poem. 'Surely', wrote his friend Frances Cornford, 'this goes far to support my contention that he was from the very first a deliberate writer!' Almost all the poetry to be found in school magazines and anthologies of children's writing is of the second kind: deliberate, precocious, literary. The purpose of this anthology is to offer the much rarer expressions of the first kind — expressions of wonder, of the 'childhood' rather than of the 'boyhood' imagination. I have borrowed these distinguishing terms from Walter de la Mare, who wrote: 'The poetical imagination is of two distinct kinds or types; the one divines, the other discovers. The one is intuitive, inductive; the other logical, deductive. The one is visionary, the other intellectual. . . . And the poet inherits, as it seems to me, the one kind from the child in him, the other from the boy in him.'

I shall consider first the kind of children's poetry I have not included. The name which is most likely to come to mind when we think of child poets is that of Marjorie Fleming. Pet Marjorie, as her friend Walter Scott called her, was born at Kirkcaldy in 1803, and died after a brief illness when she was a month under nine years old; but her poems, letters and journal have been published, her life has been written, and she has her place in the *Dictionary of National Biography*. The structure of simple verse came easily to her. Her treatment of the sonnet is decidedly free, as witness the famous one on her 'charming pug'; but she falls happily in and out of well-turned couplets in the writing of her journal. These lines from 'The Life of King James' will serve to show her technical accomplishment, her nimble wit:

1

The earl refused to do that thing
At this furious was the King.
He put his sword into his guts
And gave him many direful cuts
His vassals all to arms ran
Their leader was a cowardly man
From the field he ran with terror
I must say this was an error
He was killed by a cannon splinter
In the middle of the winter
Perhaps it was not at that time
But I could get no other ryh [rhyme].

But we can never be sure in reading Pet Marjorie's poems how far we are laughing with her or how far we are taking the liberty of laughing at her for her childish expressions of mature ideas. She belongs, not to that childhood world of dream and seclusion, but to the busy adult world that looms around her in history books and lessons. The 'most devilish' thing for her is '8 times 8 and 7 times 7 is what nature itself can't endure'. Eagerly she strives for more and still more knowledge, like the boy whose ambition was 'to think to the other end of thinking'. She gives us, not a picture of childhood through the eyes of a child, but a child's anticipation rather of the world we know. Curiosity she has in full measure; wonder she seems to lack.

And how significant is that last couplet! One of the features which may distinguish the 'boyhood' from the 'childhood' poem is the presence in the first of rhyme. At an early stage in a child's development in language he progresses from the repetitive 'baa-baa' to the rhyming 'bow-wow'. A little later he will discover the limited but for him intriguing possibilities of 'cat' and 'sat' and 'mat'. Later still he may trumpet his discovery that 'poet' rhymes with 'know it'. Somewhere along that road he may write in the manner of this six-year-old:

I mean,
Have you seen
The Queen,
All dressed in brown,
With a beautiful crown,
Sitting down
By a tree?

'No,' said he.
Later on
The day was gone,
The folk all stared
To see the Queen,
Dressed in brown,
Without a crown,
Sitting down
By a tree.
She had a cough,
The crown was off.
They gave the Queen
Some glycerine.

We may admire the poem for its ingenuity, not least in its final couplet; but the inspiration is largely verbal. So it was in the early poems of Louis MacNeice, who wrote them from the age of seven, and in later years described how. 'What I was chiefly interested in was the pattern of the words. My recipe was simple — use "thou" instead of "you" and make the ends of the lines rhyme with each other; no specific emotion or poetic content required.' By this recipe he wrote:

O parrot, thou hast grey feathers
Which thou peckest in all weathers.
And thy curled beak
Could make me squeak;
Thy tail I admire
As red as the fire
And as red as a carrot,
Thy tail I admire,
Thou cross old parrot.

Dylan Thomas, who 'had "the swan" on the brain' at that age, found that, 'luckily, there were very few rhymes for "parrot".'

In the nineteenth century, too, poets 'lisp'd in numbers', but most of their lispings were likewise of the 'boyhood' kind. Elizabeth Barrett who, in her own words, 'first mounted Pegasus' when she was four, addressed to her father at six some 'carefully indited lines' in octosyllabic couplets. By the age of twelve her future husband, Robert Browning, had composed 'enough poems to fill a volume'. Charles Kingsley wrote a 'Song Upon Life' when he was still four. Shelley was

3

only twice that age when he wrote five well-shaped six-line stanzas in defence of a cat, and even younger when he composed a satire on a French governess. Although blank verse and not rhymed was Rossetti's chosen medium at the age of five, there must have been no less deliberateness about his 'bombastic drama', *The Slave*, which was thought 'astonishingly correct' in its spelling and versification.

Rhyme, at the very least, is a jolly jingle which can delight. Thus Marjorie Hourd in her fascinating study of children's writing, *Coming Into Their Own*, quotes the ten-year-old Diane who likes 'writing verses that rhyme, because they are gay and because poetry that does not rhyme is sometimes sad and goes on and on'. Another of her poets, Hilda, prefers verse to prose, because she likes 'to put rhyming words in their place' so that she can 'make them fit in properly'. Many of the poems in this anthology rhyme: indeed, pride of place has been given to a couplet by a two-year-old which is far from mere 'bow-wow'. But, as James Britton has remarked, young children rarely succeed both in rhyming and remaining faithful to their experience; and it is clear, surely, which should be sacrificed. That there is further advantage in free verse is nowhere more convincingly shown than in the poems of Hilda Conkling, that most remarkable of child poets, of whom more later. In his Preface to her first book, *Poems by a Little Girl*, William Canton writes: 'Poets . . . will agree that this "free verse" could not have been bettered by rhyme or metre, and that in practically discarding rhyme Hilda has escaped the poetic echoes of today and yesterday.'

Gillian Hughes, who has more poems in this anthology than any other contributor, wrote one poem in a manner which recalls the deliberateness of Brooke. 'The first line was given me', she has said, 'and the principles of construction were explained. I then composed the poem while stepping out the rhythm. . . . I made no attempt to continue this form of writing in future poems.' Here is the 'stepped out' poem, written when she was seven, for contrast with her others:

> *The Country Lane*
> When I was walking down the country lane
> A sudden crispy shower of snow began to fall.
> I sheltered, snuggled in an elm-hedge cave,
> And peeped out at the pretty falling snow.

It's getting deeper, deeper now,
The trees are cold and white.
The fields are wide and lonely
Like the winter sky at night.

Teeny-weeny whitey chimneys
Smoking, sprinkle on the hills.
Smaller flakes are getting bigger,
Twirling round like balls.

Sinking in the snow
I drag my feet along the lane.
I make two trails like tram-lines,
Black footsteps home again.

This is an unfair introduction to the poet to whom, above all,
this anthology owes its being; she is not even very skilful in
her stepping! But the justification for including it, I repeat,
lies in its contrast: a sure poetic instinct led her to reject the
method.

Unlike the Marjorie Flemings and the Brookes with their
experiments, their technical ingenuity, their stepping out,
their eager reaching out for new experience, the poets of the
childhood imagination are like Coleridge's 'limber elf':

Singing, dancing to itself,
A fairy thing with red round cheeks,
That always finds, and never seeks.

Poetry for them is the expression of instinctive insight; it is
summoned from the vasty deep. It cannot be taught, indeed it
cannot even be summoned; it may only be permitted.

A poem has got to be born.
It cannot come out when you want it to;
It must be born.
When you want to make a poem you cannot
make it,
But when you do not want to make it, it comes.
(140)

Gillian Hughes was eight when she said that; she had travelled
far since her false turning. Hilda Conkling tells her mother:

I know how poems come;
They have wings;
When you are not thinking of it

5

> I suddenly say
> 'Mother, a poem!'
> Somehow I hear it
> Rustling.

Edith Sitwell gave among her hobbies in *Who's Who* 'listening to silence'. 'You know,' said a young boy, 'I always have something to do in a silence; it's like an everlasting story going on in my head.' Hilda Conkling says in another poem:

> I never know why it is
> But whenever I listen
> In flies a poem.

The poets of the childhood imagination, writes de la Mare in the essay from which I have quoted, 'live or at least desire to live in the quietude of their own spirit, in a region of which a certain order of dream seems to be a reminiscence, in a far-away listening'. Tennyson at the age of four 'heard a voice speaking in the wind'. But, though he dreamed long passages of poetry, and believed them to be good at the time, he could never remember them after waking; and the only four lines he managed to record, at the age of six, were of the 'parrot' school:

> May a cock sparrow
> Write to a barrow?
> I hope you'll excuse
> My infantile muse.

Hilda Conkling told her poems to her mother:

> If I sing, you listen;
> If I think, you know.

Mrs Conkling was so often engaged in writing that it did not seem strange if she scribbled while her daughter spoke them. Sometimes a poem would be written down later from memory and read back to the child, who always remembered if it was not exactly in its original form. Young children's poetry must often be recorded in this way. The five-year-old who has learnt to write is unlikely to be able to write quickly enough to keep pace with ideas. A six-year-old girl, who had recently recovered from serious eye trouble, was resting in bed when a poem came to her. Many years later she has recalled: 'I was overcome by its tragic beauty. I tried to write it down, but I was just learning to spell, and the original manuscript is somewhat bizarre, and never did, even then, convey my almost mystical feeling of the poem's truth.' Here is the original version together with the author's transliteration:

> See Not
> See. not.
> my. yz
> cloz.
> See. not.
> the. sun.
> See. not.
> the. moon.
> or. the. strs.
> that. run.
> See. not
> my cher.
> See. not
> no. but
> the. cooc.coo
> so. ne.

> See Not
> See not my eyes close,
> See not the sun,
> See not the moon
> Or the stars that run.
> See not my tear,
> See not, no!
> But the cuckoo so near.

Not every five-year-old is as gifted a speller as the young Rossetti. In the poems I have collected spellings have been normalized for at least one obvious reason: that those spelt as written by children would seem unduly naïve in contrast to those written down by grown-ups.

In his Foreword to *The Janitor's Boy*, William Rose Benét compares favourably its young author, Nathalia Crane, with Hilda Conkling. 'Hilda is a real poet. But she has never grappled with and conquered certain problems of poetic structures for which Miss Crane, by sheer instinct, seems to have wrested occasional victory.' What the elder poet should really be remarking is not a difference in quality or achievement but a difference in kind: quite simply, Nathalia Crane's are poems of the 'boyhood', Hilda Conkling's of the 'child-hood' imagination. Moreover, while it is rare to find in children's poetry of either kind evidence of tension between form and content, even Hilda Conkling, whose poems fly in, could be aware of the 'intolerable struggle':

> When moonlight falls on the water
> It is like fingers touching the chords of a harp
> On a misty day.
> When moonlight strikes the water
> I cannot get it into my poem:
> I only hear the tinkle of ripplings of light.
> When I see the water's fingers and the moon's
>   rays
> Intertwined,
> I think of all the words I love to hear,
> And try to find words white enough
> For such shining. . . .

Compare, too, the experience of the seven-year-old Edward Hogg (103). Sometimes the struggle to express is the means of establishing the truth of an experience, as in this poem by an eight-year-old American boy:

> When I want to write a poem about snow
> I think — how does it fall?
> And why do we play in it?
> I think hard and hard.
> Every time I think hard and harder!
>
> I get the Idea
> I get to understand it
> I feel it in my heart.
> That is how I make the snow come true. (141)

The boy is expressing, surely, a common experience: that we do not know what we think till we hear what we say.

Nor should we infer from Gillian Hughes's account of a poem's coming that the promptings come only from within. In the eight-year-olds' section of the anthology I have included four short poems on 'The Fountain' (146-9) which were written at a teacher's suggestion by members of the same class. Another teacher, seeking a few moments' peace in a class of six-year-olds, asked them to close their eyes and make up a poem about a dandelion. One of the small girls said:

> I had a little dandelion
> As yellow as could be;
> I put him in some water
> And then he smiled at me.

Next day one of the small boys said that he had thought of a second verse:

> But oh as he got older
> His hair began to grow
> And seeds grew at the bottom
> And I blew them, every one.

The novelist, Neil Bell, sent me in 1963 the following quatrain, 'written in my classroom forty years ago by an eight-year-old boy':

> On the hill
> There is a mill
> But the mill is still
> For the man is ill.

My correspondent added: 'It has always seemed to me a perfect poem of its kind, conveying in short and simple words, in their best order, a clear and poignant image of an event or circumstance.' For teachers who encourage — permit — free writing in their classes such instances will be matched in their experience. Marjorie Hourd is one among many who have shown how the right conditions can be set up and with what benefit. Her premise is Wordsworthian: 'To some extent, at least, every man is by birth a poet', she says in *Coming Into Their Own*. In an earlier book, *The Education of the Poetic Spirit*, she suggests that the teacher 'bring into a whole the realities and desires, thoughts and phantasies, rebellions and submissions, good and bad, which he finds in the material before him'. To do so requires something akin to Wordsworth's 'wise passiveness', to Keats's 'diligent Indolence' and 'Negative Capability'. The teacher, she says, must practise 'the technique of knowing and yet appearing not to know'. Such a gift is clearly possessed by the poet and teacher, Charles Causley, who contributes so valuably to this book. If the poems I have collected serve to support such work in the classroom, and to encourage other teachers to practise it, I could not be more delighted. At the same time I must make clear that in collecting and presenting them I have not been primarily concerned with education or child psychology. I

make a higher claim for the poems: that they deserve atten-
tion, not as specimens still less as models, but for their own
sake.

Even a quite young child can express literary aspirations:

> I wish I were a poet to write a lot of poems
> I'd be like William Shakespeare and John Long-
> fellow [sic]
> But all these wishes shall come to nothing
> For as you see I am only a schoolboy.

No less literary, though more confident in tone, is this:

> A poet must have a good imagination
> Like Shakespeare
> He should have satisfaction from his creation.

Such aspirations raise the question of how far we may admit
as 'childhood' poetry that which is obviously derivative. In
his Introduction to a very different sort of anthology, *Poems
by Children, 1950-1961*, Michael Baldwin suggests that 'we
don't know nearly enough about the sort of creative near-
ecstasy in which a young adolescent can parody and even
plagiarize'. In his excellent book, *Rose, Where Did You Get
That Red?*, the American Kenneth Koch expounds his method
of 'teaching great poetry to children' by teaching the reading
of poetry and the writing of it as one subject. His success in
doing this can be measured by the pupils' poems which he
quotes, some of them showing true originality, and all of
them an awareness of experiences which the pupils have
made their own. They serve as heartening ratification of
Keats: 'We find fine things but never feel them to the full
until we have gone the same steps as the author.' Michael
Baldwin also suggests, in the course of some tail-chasing
argument about the 'innocent voice', that to be true to one's
experience may be a misleadingly adult concept: 'children
can be true in a different way and to a wider range of feeling
than we can. It is easier . . . for them to be true to the artifi-
cial, the phantasmagoric, and the dream, and to come freshly
to ideas that an adult would conceive only as a result of deliberate intention.' Thus Wordsworth's six years' Darling
shakes with 'newly learned art' the 'fragment from his dream
of human life'; the little actor cons another part —

> As if his whole vocation
> Were endless imitation.

Interestingly, as we learn from Charles Lamb, William Wordsworth junior 'seemeth to keep aloof from any source of
imitation, and purposely to remain ignorant of what mighty
poets have done in this kind before him; for, being asked if
his father had ever been on Westminster Bridge, he answered
that he did not know!' Children learn by imitation; there
would be no poems in this anthology — perhaps in all literature — if those that were in some part derivative had been
excluded. At the same time I have omitted poems in which
the child has too obviously mimicked an adult voice, for he
cannot then, it seems to me, be true to his own. As an
example, a poem in Hilda Conkling's second book, *Shoes of
the Wind*, begins:

> When the south sang like a nightingale
> It was the hour bringing the tinted dawn.
> Over the meadow's grassy breast
> I trod with trembling feet.

We feel here that the poet is trying on her party dress —
indeed, she is trying on someone else's.

Sometimes a poem may be reshaped by an older hand.
'The Stream', which appears in its original form in the anthology (159), was altered by the poet's mother to:

> I love to see the stream
> Upon a summer's day.
> I like to see it sparkling
> With the river running by,
> The trout with varied colours
> That shine beneath the sky.

Sometimes the child may revise the original after a period of
time. 'The Moonlight Horses' (206) was written when Lalage
Prime was eight. Two years later she revised it for publication
in the *Young Elizabethan*. Here are verses three to six:

> They whinny for joy
> When the moon shines bright
> And jump off the roundabout
> Into the night.
>
> They trot through the village
> And out on the moor,
> The bushes are covered
> With silvery hoar.

They meet elfin ponies
And with them they dance,
Their silvery hooves flashing
As swiftly they prance.

Then they gallop back home
Up the pebbly lane
Then up on the roundabout,
Wooden again.

We note the greater proficiency of technique: we recognize, as did the ten-year-old, that 'does rise' in verse three of the original is a poeticism; but is not the concluding line of that verse preferable by far to its revision? 'Sniffing a lily' may have been prompted by rhyme, but it has a freshness which has been sacrificed in 'silvery hoar' and 'elfin'.

Influence should work in the opposite direction. The Persian poet, Kahlil Gibran, wrote of children:

You can give them your love, but not your
thoughts,
For they have their own thoughts.
You can house their bodies, but not their souls,
For their souls dwell in the house of tomorrow.
You can strive to be like them,
But seek not to make them like you,
For life goes not backward, nor tarries with
yesterday.

'The Child is father of the Man', and his most precious gift is his sense of wonder.

I keep wondering through and through my
heart
Where all the beautiful things in the world
Come from
And while I wonder
They go on being beautiful.

The man may lose this gift of wonder; a seven-year-old laments:

Alas the people just walk past
As if my little daisy
They'd never, never seen. (134)

But the child may teach him to regain it, for he sees newly. He has, as C. Day Lewis once said, an advantage over the

INTRODUCTION

professional writer, for his 'experiences, though often bewil-
dering, are not yet staled by over-repetition, nor smudged by
preconceptions, nor thinned by abstractions'. His soul indeed,
as John Earle writes in *Micro-Cosmographie*, 'is yet a white
paper unscribled with observations of the world, wherewith
at length it becomes a blurr'd Note-booke'. Sometimes the
paper is so 'unscribled' that his spontaneous utterances
show no consciousness that others have not seen things as
he sees them. At other times, like the seven-year-old just
quoted, he may be aware of his privilege. Wiedeman Browning,
the son of Robert and Elizabeth Barrett, who was unable to
pronounce his name and called himself Penini, one day made
this poem:

> The willow is a green fountain.
> None hath called it a green fountain
> But only Penini.

At the age of three, his mother tells, he is 'an enthusiast in
nature, and descants upon the "red trees" (he calls anything
red which has any sort of colour) and the "beautiful sun,
which God hangs up on a nail".' At five, 'Penini is always
en verve. He's always ready to make a poem on any subject,
and doesn't ask you to wait while he clears his voice.'

Children, it goes without saying, use words newly. Andrew
Marvell pictures his 'Little T.C.':

> In the green Grass she loves to lie,
> And there with her fair Aspect tames
> The Wilder flow'rs, and gives them names.

It is true, as Michael Baldwin argues, that for a young child
'one word is as fresh as another': that one child can write 'my
beautiful-eyed bunny' with as much wonder as another who
writes 'my bun-eyed bunny' or 'my braille-eyed bunny'. It is
true also that, for the child, 'bunny' itself may be a whole
poem. But the recognition that for a child no word can be
stale should not cause us to reject what freshness it may com-
municate, albeit by chance. 'When a child speaks of honey as
bee jam', says the Dorset poet William Barnes, 'it reveals the
creation of language'. When he speaks of thunder as 'Bumble-
a-bumble-a-bum' or of bacon frying as 'slitterling and slatt-
ling', it reveals one of the sources of poetry. And how otherwise should we speak of 'tumble-storm' for waterfall, or
'crumby road' for gravel path?

13

The last two coinings come from a delightful book, *The Sayings of the Children*, published in 1918 and now too little known. In it Pamela Glenconner has recorded such sayings of her children as:

'I took off the top, and I only just put in the spoon, and all the egg came caterpillaring out.'

'Then I saw Mummy come in with a rather frog-smiling lady.'

[Of dreams] 'The picture book of the night.'

[Of thinking] 'Nothing but air, speaking in your heart.'
Many of these are the stuff of poetry; another rather different anthology might be composed of them — every family should keep one. Such definitions as 'Today is tomorrow from yesterday' and 'Shy means that you don't know anybody at first' — these from a four-year-old — deserve to be remembered.

Some men a forward motion love,
But I by backward steps would move
writes Henry Vaughan; and he and the poets of a childhood imagination — Wordsworth, Coleridge, Blake, Traherne, the dreamers, mystics, visionaries — have known the value of these backward steps. Vaughan's happiness in his 'Angell-infancy' is echoed by Traherne:

How like an Angel came I down!
And no one has expressed more perceptively than Wordsworth that time of infancy when 'heaven lies about us'. I hope that this anthology, which records the shared experience of childhood, will help its readers to recollect, and to relive.

GENERAL NOTE ON
THE POEMS

The poems are arranged in seven age groups, from Two years to Eight years, and roughly by subject within each group. With two exceptions they are as spoken or written: from 'The Robin' (16) some lines have been omitted; 'In the Summer' (94) is the final couplet only of a longer poem. As explained in the Introduction, spellings have been normalized. In the comparatively few cases where there were no titles, these have been supplied. For the first nineteen poems and for about half the remainder, individual notes are provided on pp. 000 – 000. Many of these notes are of especial interest, but to have printed them with the poems, or even to have indicated them with asterisks, would have seemed an intrusion.

TWO YEARS

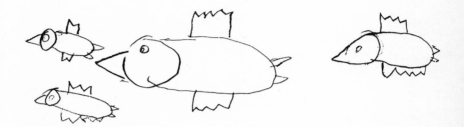

Starlings, by Ian Bolsover age 7

1   **BELLS**

Bells are ringing,
Frances is singing.

                           Frances Kent

2   **LADYBIRDS IS HORRID**

Hushabye, hushabye, it's dark in the
             morning,
Flowers are up in the sky.
Mama's my baby, my little, little
             baby;
Thomas smells of flowers.
Sing a song, sing a song, sing a song.

                        Lucinda Broadbent

3   **BU'FLY**

Bu'fly, bu'fly
Fell in a pond
Why spider, why spider, why?

                        Thomas Broadbent

4   **STARLINGS**

This cold grey winter afternoon
The starlings
On the television aerial
Look like sultanas
On a stalk.

                    Lucy Hosegood

5   SNOWMAN

You must stay here
Till the snow melts away
Into the road.

When the snow comes
I will go into the garden
And make a snowman.
And I will make a snow hand
And hold it.
And I will make snow feet
And he can walk about in the garden.
And when the snow melts,
He will blow away in the wind.

Ben Howison

6   MR DYE

Mr Dye
Lost his tie
While he was walking along.
He went upstairs
And found his tie,
And then he put it on.
And then he sang a song.

Christopher Parish

A SORT OF GIRAFFE

Kangaroo, kangaroo,
I'm a sort of Giraffe.
If I eat all the branches
The birds have to fly in the clouds.

Timothy Broadbent

THREE YEARS

Dancing, by Claire Wilson age 5

8   LULLABY

Hush! Hush! the misty music
On the far bony hills of Japan.

Peter Simpson

9   ON BODMIN MOOR

The owl is the mother of the dark,
And the moon comes up
From under the mud.

Patrick Buxton

10   A RAINBOW

Blue and white
All tangled up together.
It was in the sky,
But it wasn't part of the sky,
Because it went out of the sky
Sooner or later.

Gillian Hughes

11   BEN LEDI

Ben Ledi you are covered with snow.
I shall take it off you,
Then I shall make a snowman.
After I shall put some moss on you.

Rebecca Thomson

12   BONNING ABOUT

Bonning about
Bonning about
In Copenhagen bonning about
Jesus wanted to bonning about
But Mary and Joseph said no
Christ the Lord.

                          Catherine Askew

13   THE PRINCESS

I will be the princess
Sitting on a gold and silver tree
A Christmas tree —
So will you come with me?

                          Anna Machin

The Princess, by Anna Winstanley age 3

SILVER POLAR BEARS

It was such a lovely day,
They slept in the garden
And the children smiled asleep
And the birds were laughing up in the
        sky.
. . . .
They ran up, they ran down,
They ran secret in the town,
They couldn't stop, they couldn't stop,
They ran up and down the shop.
And the silver polar bears,
They *did* enjoy it!

                              Roberta Nesham

15   THE BUTTERFLIES' SONG

Oh! the butterflies in the moonshine!
And the daisies in the moonshine!
And the red lights in the darkness!

16   THE ROBIN

Once there was a Jolly Robin
In the winter cold and frosty night
And the owl 'Too-witta Woo
And that's all'
Said the owl to the horse in the barn.

And when the stars shine bright
Over the hills the clouds were bright
He didn't know the right
That's all
You see.

THE ROBIN

The owl lived with the jolly robin
        once
When he saw over the clouds he was
        certainly right
In the day time CREW
That's all.

Once when he had a cough
Had a cough so ill,
When he had to have a doctor
Took his temperature too.
But when he got up and wasn't ill
Any more

He went outside, drove on the
        motorbike,
On the motorcar too.
When it said a STEEP hill
They went down — bumpety bump
Over the hill they ran all night.

They went over bumps and bumps
        and bumps
And HOTHERNED and right.
There's notes and notes and notes.
. . . .
When the landscape came inside
When all the animals were inside the
        house
So they drank some water
From he grabbed a sardine tight
And he mended the roof of the house
With a hammer
That's all.

Once there was a jolly robin redbreast
The mountains were in the
        SCARLATAN
Said to the motorcar too — somesing

THE ROBIN

Then they couldn't have
Then they couldn't . . . in the
Christmas deep
VIOLET.

When the puffer train blew on his
            whistle
The puffer train blew so hard.
When on the mountain steep
The SCREEP and the SCREEP.
That's all.

When the violet grew
The violet grew through the mountain
It pushed the mountain through.
                              Hugh Bradford

17   THE LOLLIPOP

God dropped his lollipop
From the sky,
And somebody caught it
In a little pie.
                      Garnet Frost

29

FOUR YEARS

Little Mouse, by Claire Houdret age 4

18   THE BROOK DANCE

There is going to be the sound of bells
And murmuring.
This is the brook dance:
There is going to be the sound of
         voices,
And the smallest will be the brook:
It is the song of water
You will hear.
A little winding song
To dance to . . . .

                Hilda Conkling

19   THE WONDERFUL SINGER

I am a wonderful singer
And so are you
I will sweep the kitchen
And sing to you.

                Nancy Davies

20   THE WIND

'Whump!' goes the wind on the
         window,
And the window goes 'Whamp!'

21   O HAPPY HOURS

O happy hours, O happy hours,
In the garden with the flowers!

                Charles Wintringham

22   TO A FLOWER

Sparkle up, little tired flower
Leaning in the grass!

Did you find the rain of night
Too heavy to hold?

Hilda Conkling

A Flower, by Katie Alford age 6

23   NIGHT

It is cold
On the wold
And the foxes at nights
In the houses see lights.

Mary Hemming

THE SEA

Look, look at the ruffling tuffling sea!
I am going to throw a stone
Into the throat of a wave.

Martin Panter

25   **LOVE**

I had a little duck
And he swam away
I had a little chicky
And he was too noisy
And he ran away.

I had a little horsey
And he ran away.
I wanted a little lamb
And it came last.
I wanted a lamb
And it didn't run away.

It put things where I wanted them
And I was awfully pleased
And I like it and it's going to keep
            with me;
And I love it and I love it and I love it
And it loves me.

Jane Simon

THE LITTLE MOUSE

Once upon a time there was a little
                mouse
Crawling along the floor.
I said to him, 'Where are you going?'
And he hid behind the door.

                              Nancy Davies

The Little Mouse, by Kathryn Witts age 4

UNDER THE LID

A pack of scraffled cards,
A box of animals,
And far a bigger box containing
                blocks
Lie underneath this lid.
Next a train that once ran on a line.
It will again some day
And see the signals as it flashes by.
A tiny scribbled notebook lies within
It sighs anew — a third box — but
                inside
Blank pages — books — cash notes —
                addresses signed
And over all the lid. CRASH!

                              Dorothy Wilson

SUNDAY

Sunday is an awkward day.
Of course it is God's own.

Alison Buxton

SATELLITE

No one knows how to
Unlock the mystery of the satellite
The way it bounds into the sky
It is like a beaming star

It settles silently
And as it settles
People all over the world wonder.

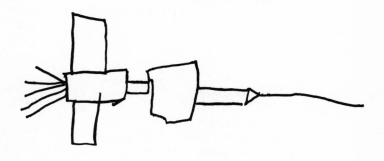

The Satellite, by Jonathan Lyford age 4

POEM AT BEDTIME

My heart is beating
And the Lord is near me.

Richard Ashworth

31 GOD

God is good,
As good as water.
He loves me,
And I love him.

Lucinda Broadbent

32 CAROL

Mary has a baby,
She holds it in her hands.
The baby's a nice one — she wants to
        keep it.
Joseph sits on the doorstep
Keeping very still.

Lucinda Broadbent

33 LUCY'S CAROL

When the Baby borned
Joseph said to Mary,
'What am I going to do about
This Little-born Jesus Baby Christ?
I never knew it was going to be like
        this,
With all these angels and kings
And shepherds and stars and things;
It's got me worried, I can tell you,
On Christmas Day in the morning.'

Mary said to Joseph,
'Not to worry, my darling,
Dear old darling Joseph;
Everything's going to be all right,
Because the Angel told me not to fear;

38

LUCY'S CAROL

So just hold up the lamp,
So I can see the dear funny sweet
      little face
Of my darling Little-born Jesus Baby
      Christ.'

Joseph said to Mary,
'Behold the handy-man of the Lord!'

Happy Christmas, happy Christmas!
Christ is born today.

                        Lucy

34   **AFTER**

After war time
It's spring time.

FIVE YEARS

Little Birds, by Brett Dowell age 5

35   LOVE

I love you as much as gold.
I love you like silver and clear glass,
Like bright brass and diamonds.
Nobody has ever loved anyone so
         much as I love you.
It gives me a lovely feeling in my
         heart.

I will live with you all my days.
And when I am an old man I will look
         after you,
Because I love you.

                       Leonard Gray

36   MONOLOGUE

I want to believe in God,
But I want to be rich.
If you're rich you don't believe in
         God.

I don't believe in God.
I don't believe in Daddy,
I don't believe in Mummy,
I don't believe in brothers or sisters.

But I'm a sister;
That means I don't believe in myself.

                   Sally de Berker

37   GOD

God is so lovely,
God is the sky,
God is the dearest man in the world,
I'd like to marry that man,
God, do come down.

Sally de Berker

38   CLOUDS AND SUN

Look at the sun,
It follows us all the time,
It's God's head,
I expect that's what it is.
I can see his hand,
When he puts out the sun,
God's hand.

Sally de Berker

39   NIGHT

D'you know the moon is shining at
                    night?
And all the stars are shining like
                    might,
And all the people that sleep at night.
And all the wind comes running
                    through.
And sometimes the rain comes down
                    at night
And comes trickling through the sky.

WHAT IS WATER?

The world turns softly
Not to spill its lakes and rivers.
The water is held in its arms
And the sky is held in the water.
What is water,
That pours silver,
And can hold the sky?

Hilda Conkling

41   BY LAKE CHAMPLAIN

I was as bare as a leaf
And I felt the wind on my shoulder.
The trees laughed
When I picked up the sun in my
                    fingers.
The wind was chasing the waves,
Tangling their white curls.
'Willow trees,' I said,
'O willows,
Look at your lake!
Stop laughing at a little girl
Who runs past your feet in the sand!'

Hilda Conkling

42   THE HAPPY MOON

The happy moon does shine over the
                    wide earth,
Down the lane where the little boy
                    runs,
Over the wide desert where the camels
                    go
Humpity, humpity, humpity . . . .

Ian Liston

When I see the stars
The moon is shining bright.
I often see the blue blue sky
And trees all round.
Green leaves and brown leaves
Twinkling away
They're usually awake
Birds are twittering
On the trees
And all flowers are out
And all the flowers.
I'll show you them.
Bluebells and roses
Buttercups and daisies
Primroses and poppies
Green grass and all those things
Things like snapdragons
Wallflowers and things like that
Daffodils and crocuses
Lilies and those, all of them
Awake in summer.

Even poppies bright and red
Everything you can possibly think of,
All of them will do.

Even pansies purplish colour
All of them will do
Including dandelion.
All of them are out.

                                    Sally Young

44   THE VIOLET

Blue sky over the green,
No one peeps in between
These leaves at me.
Yet for all to see
I am as clear as you,
Little bird in the blue.

                 Julia Moreton

45   LITTLE BIRD

Oh little bird, little bird
I love to hear your song
The sweetest sounds I ever heard
That make me happy all day long.
Oh sing to me always
Please, dear little bird
All through the summer days
So I can learn your happy words.

                      Nicola

A Little Bird, Alexandra Court age 5

OH, MRS CHICKEN!

Oh, oh, oh, Mrs Chicken!
Your egg is beginning to crack.
It opened out wide
There was nothing inside,
So we put it away in the shack.

Garnet Frost

DUCK

Duck Duck Duck
Swimming on the pond
Tell me how you swim along
Duck Duck Duck
Swimming on the pond.

Judith Stinton

Duck, Sarah Winckless age 5

DUCK LEGS

I love to see the rippling stream
Going through the summer
With the duck swimming on it
With the white feathers soft.
The rippling stream
The rippling stream
How I love to see it sailing
With the ducks with their legs off
And the chicks come out with their
                chicken legs.

                          Janet Savage

49   MOUSE

Little mouse in grey velvet,
Have you had a cheese-breakfast?
There are no crumbs on your coat,
Did you use a napkin?
I wonder what you had to eat,
And who dresses you in grey velvet?
                          Hilda Conkling

Mouse, by Sophie Hardwicke age 4

LITTLE MR BUZZLY FLY

Little Mr Buzzly Fly
Very quickly passes by,
Leaves his footmarks on the pane,
Up the glass and down again.

Valery Haggie

Buzzly Fly, by Juliette MacVarish age 6

51   A WISH

I wish that I could fly
High high up in the sky
Over the roof-tops over the towns
Over the meadows and over the downs
Right up to the moon!
Then come down again;
Soon soon soon.

Judith Stinton

52   THE SNOWMAN

A scarf round his neck
A broom in his hand,
A little snow nose
And two bits of coal
For his little black eyes,
Some holly in his hat,
A big black hat;
I made a snowman
By the garden gate.

53   THE BONFIRE

Bonfire! Bonfire!
Oh! How exciting!
Under the starlit sky;
Bonfire! Bonfire!

Helen Dovey

54   GUY FAWKES AND OTHERS

Guy Fawkes has a hat,
Two little sharp eyes.
He burns on the bonfire
On a frosty night.

Santa Claus has lots of toys.
He has a great big sack on his back.
He has crackers.
He might have balloons.
Christmas is lovely in a winter's night.

I have a ship.
It sails in the bath.
It sails to the other side.
It has a funnel.
I pretend smoke comes out.
It sails in the bath tonight.

55   THE CHRISTMAS TREE

Oh my little Christmas tree,
The curtains are not shut yet.
Wait until my daddy comes
And makes the windows dark . . . .

                                      Ian Gray

A Christmas Tree, by Seonaid Cook age 5

56   CHRISTMAS

I watch the star,
Eye to eye,
From my window
As I lie.

Quentin Neill

57   SCHOOL

Oh! What a pity!
One so looks forward to school!
All one's life! One's whole life!
And oh! Mummy, it is nothing
But disappointment.
I can hardly bear it.

Lucy Hosegood

School, by Darren Pitcher age 6

58   COLD

So cold in the night
When it sleets and snows;
So cold in the night
When the north wind blows;
So cold in the night
As cold as can be;
So cold in the night
For you and me.

Valerie Ormond

59   THE WIND

Whistling whistling
Blowing blowing
Branches swaying
Blossom blowing
The wind.

Rosemary Stinton

60   AUTUMN

It is such a breeze in autumn.
The rain falls down on cloudy days,
And the hail stones jump about the
        grass.
And now it's coming colder and
        colder and colder
And colder until it's WINTER.

Hugh Bradford

61   SNOWFLAKES

Oh you pretty snowflake
Dropping from the sky
Like a bit of whitewash
Nice and clean and dry!

                Nancy Davies

62   THE CLOCK

When I wake I hear the clock
Going tick tock, tick tock, tick tock.
Sometimes it's saying get up get up
Feed your pup feed your pup
Sometimes it's saying get dressed get
            dressed
My idea's the best the best
Sometimes I say, 'Yes old clock',
Tick tock tick tock tick tock tick
            tock.

                Judith Stinton

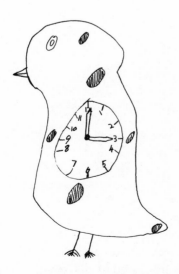

The Clock, by Scott Briggs age 7

DANCING

I like to go to dancing.
I dance upon my toes.
I wear some pretty frocks.
I'll show you how my dance goes.

Barbara

Dancing, by Nina Lammiman age 5

64   **THE SINGER**

When I shout and when I sing
I am like a tulip singing in the sky.

Jocelyn Lomer

SIX YEARS

Dandelion, by Diane Hipwell age 6

65   HAPPINESS

All my days have been happy ones.
I am to be Lord Mayor in the
        Lanimers.
Tomorrow I will wear my robes, blue
        velvet and a gold chain.

Tonight I won sixpence in a race.
The Provost spoke to me, and let me
        touch his chain,
Gold, like mine.

I sing in the choir, and wear a surplice,
I am known to the police.

My life has been so happy I can hardly
        bear it.
When I die, I hope they will say this
        of me,
'He was an important man.'
                    Leonard Gray

66   THE FACE

I know a face, a lovely face;
As full of beauty as of grace,
A face of pleasure, ever bright
In utter darkness it gives light.
A face that is itself like Joy,
To have seen it I'm a lucky boy,
But I've a joy that have few other,
This lovely woman is my MOTHER.
               E. Wyndham Tennant

I'm putting Mummy's stockings on.
Daddy will laugh.
They are awfully long for me.
I think I must look funny.
I'm going to a party!

They do not match.
One's a bit too long.
One's a bit too short.
One looks like a silk one.
They feel awfully wriggly,
Like caterpillars all down my legs.
I think they do look funny.

I'm putting Mummy's shoes on.
Plonk! Plonk! Plonk! Plonk!
Walking round the room,
I'm going to a party.
I couldn't go outside like this!

I'm putting Mummy's coat on.
I'm going to the theatre!
The fur feels soft and warm on my
                        chin.
No one can see my stockings;
My coat comes to my toes.

Ha! Ha! Ha!
The sleeves are too long.
They flap up and down, up and down,
As I move my arms, jigging them up
                        and down.
Ha! Ha! Ha!
I expect I look funny.

I have to roll up my sleeves
To get to my hands, to put my hat on.
I'm putting Mummy's hat on.
Do I look nice?

Walking round and round the room,
Slopping my heels up and down,
With my sleeves flapping like birds'
                                    wings,
Round and round,
I'm going to the theatre.

                                    Gillian Hughes

68   MY BATH

When I lie in my light green bath at
                        night
Under the warm velvety water,
I make shadows with my fingers,
And splash to make the waves.
The water feels like velvet on my
                        body.

I stay in the bath too long.
My fingers get creased and pleated.
I touch the water tap.
It makes me cold.
I let the water out.
K-K-K-K KORR -W-W!
K-K-K-K KORR-W-W!
I have got to get out of the bath
Until tomorrow.

                                    Gillian Hughes

69   **EVERYTHING BELONGS TO**
           SOMETHING ELSE IF YOU THINK
           ABOUT IT

O the towel and the bath
And the bath and the soap,
And the soap was the fat,
And the fat was the pig,
And the pig was the bran,
And the bran makes sausages;
And man eats the sausages
And God gets man.

                 E. Wyndham Tennant

70   **BED**

In my nice cosy bed I lie,
Snuggling down cuddly and cumfy,
On a dark frosty night,
Shivery cold.
I snuggle under Mummy's arm,
And say my prayers.
I lie and watch the pattern
Of my night-light on the ceiling.
I watch the white and blacky shadows,
And pretend that someone's
Scraping my ceiling clean.
Then it's morning.

                 Gillian Hughes

71   **A DREAM**

I had a dreadful dream last night.
All the trees were bending over the
               bridge.
I looked, and all the trees by the river
               had grown huge,
And they curved over the bridge.

A DREAM

I said, 'Mummy, we can't go through
            that big forest,
We shall have to go over the other
            bridge.'
And when I woke up, I still thought I
            should have to say,
'Mummy, we can't go through that big
            forest,
We shall have to go over the other
            bridge.'

                          Gillian Hughes

72   DANDELION

I've got a dandelion
It is yellow.
I've got a father
He's such a happy fellow.
I've got a bowl
It's very very big
Every time I see it
It makes me jig.

                    Hilary Shaw

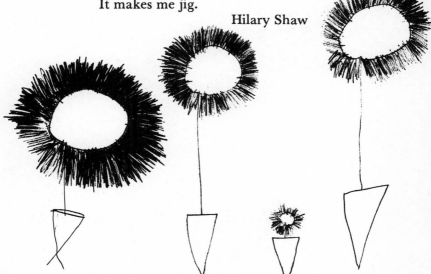

Dandelions, by Emma Jones age 6

63

BALLERINA

It's doing a ballet dance
With its lovely dress,
Yellow, blue, green and red.
Dancing on its tip-toes;
Round and round
Waltzing;
Spinning to the corner;
Waving invisible arms;
Wobbling;
Bowing;
Finishing with a quavering dance,
And sitting with a curtsy.
My spinning top!
A table for the stage!

Gillian Hughes

Ballerina, by Beverley Price age 5

74   AUNT JEAN

Happy Christmas, Aunt Jean
Do you know that we have been
Looking forward very much
To your gentle touch?

                    Richard Buxton

75   CALM

No wind:
Not a tree blowing:
No leaves on the trees:
Bare old branches.
It's ever so quiet
Without a tree blowing.

                    Gillian Hughes

76   QUIET

As quiet as night
As quiet as a pencil writing
As quiet as a doll sleeping
As quiet as a baby drinking his bottle.

77   LULLABY

I will sing you a lullaby
And if — if — if
The lullaby lasts
I will sing you another.

LULLABY

And the lullaby did last
But it lasted too long for the baby
For it went fast asleep
Before the lullaby was finished.
That pleased the mother most awfully.

Richard Armstrong

78   CHRISTMAS CAROL

Little Boy Baby
Lying in the straw,
Cuddly and cosy,
Warm and snug.
'Where is your Mother, little Baby?
She is leaning by your side.
She'll pick you up and nurse you
If the straw pricks you,
And makes you cry.'

Gillian Hughes

79   SNOW FALLING

A white newspaper sky
Ruled out for writing
With telephone wires
For the lines!
A sky full of snow flakes!

The snow looks like dust
Coming down;
Snow-dust,
Diving round and round
And down
All the little snow flakes
Are falling to pieces

66

SNOW FALLING

So small that they are blown
The way of the breeze
Before they land.
Snow on the seat
Looks like sugar sprinkled.
Large flakes fall softly
And slowly to the ground.

A blackbird, with orange beak
Is sitting on the path
Feeling the snow.
Birds at a distance
Look like little round balls,
Black balls rolling along the sky.

Now the snow is coming quicker.
Snow flakes play 'Follow-my-leader',
Running round and round in a ring
Like a circus.
Now slowly
Like strings of cotton
Threaded to round snow buttons.

Gillian Hughes

80   ## FROST

Everything looks beautiful
As if snow's on the ground.
Cobwebs hanging
Like tinsel on a Christmas Tree!
Frost cobwebs like woven lace
On the fence!
A robin sits on a white tree
Tickling its wings.
All is quiet and still.

Gillian Hughes

Beautiful is the sun
Like a real summer day;
The scent of holidays in the air!
Mist on the Cotswolds, whitey blue:
Trees on top;
Trees that look puffed up!
And woods in the distance!
Hundreds of elms stand straight and
          still
In fields and woods.
A hedge like a black cat's fur
Makes a corner on a hill field.
A haystack half fallen
Stands on the grass.
Pigeons silvery and black
Fly up and down
On to the Indian brown earth
Of a tidy field.
A little path
Through a ploughed field
Leads to nowhere.
Goats nibble at the grass
By the roadside.
A bird hops about on the dry earth.
Sheep in a meadow look like sacks.
Cows rest.
A bonfire smokes.

                    Gillian Hughes

82   SUMMER

A hot dreary sky heavy with heat;
Still hot air;
No breeze anywhere.
White butterflies, flying in twos,
Flutter their wings
Turning corners in the air,
Landing,

Quarrelling,
Busily working!
Flittering from one flower to another,
And then, away.
The sun comes from behind a cloud,
Hot, scorching, gleaming sun.
The aspen glitters.
Lombardy poplars,
Half dark green, half light,
Hot and sticky, as if they could feel
            the heat,
Are fanning slowly.
And I swing on for ever and ever.

                              Gillian Hughes

83   LOMBARDY POPLAR

Lombardy poplar
Worshipping God
Singing to praise
All trees and amaze
The trees which do watch
The praising so merrily
The Lombardy poplar sings.

                              Crispin Pickles

84   WINTER ELMS

Better than summer trees
I like the curved branches,
And pretty curling twigs
Of heavy winter elms;
Horny twigs,
Like crispy hair grown long and curly
On a horse's forehead,
A few leaves, brown and crackly,
Clutch to the branches of the trees,
Not wanting to fall.

                   Gillian Hughes

85   WEEPING WILLOWS

I like the ugly winter willows,
Drooping willows,
With their loosely hanging branches;
Like hay blown loose
On the top of a hay-stack;
Like the ginger wig of a clown's head.

                   Gillian Hughes

86   WINTER RAIN

The trees are dripping wet
As the rain comes galloping down
Making all the plants droop their
          leaves.

The lawn is sloppy.
The horrid cold rain makes rings in
          the puddles
As it drops.

WINTER RAIN

Raindrops like silver sweets,
Silver balls of water,
Glass berries,
Clutch to the bare branches of the
                apple tree,
Falling one at a time.
And more come to take their place.
                        Gillian Hughes

87   RAIN

All the little diamonds are falling from
                the sky,
Falling, falling, falling without a single
                sound.
You must never worry if you've
                nothing to do,
Just go into the garden and see what
                you can do.
                        Clare Wright

88   TREES AND CLOUDS

I like to listen to the trees
And the nice noise they make,
The wish-wish noise.
And I like to look at the clouds
When they move and make
                patterns.
                        Roger Cohen

89   POND AT EVENING

The sun lies down
The trees are blowing
And they howled and howled and
        howled and howled and
                howled
And a fish popped up
And said 'Bobby-nut'
And bubbled into a pond.

90   FIRE FAIRIES

Dancing up the chimney
Up to church they go,
Faster faster up they go,
Dancing out of sight.
Till they turn to soot again,
Into church we say.

                        Clare Wright

91   THE FIRE

See the yellow flames appearing,
And of course there is the hearing
Of the yellow flames alive,
Buzzing, always buzzing
As a busy bee-hive.

                        Valerie Ormond

BUSY BEE

'Busy bee! Busy bee!
I hear your voice of humming.'

'There I see my hive
And a flower that I may get the pollen
from.'

'Busy bee! Busy bee!
Where will you go to next
Busy bee?'

'I shall go to a garden
And find some roses.
Then what shall I do?
I shall fly off home,
And sit down and make some honey
This afternoon.'

Gillian Hughes

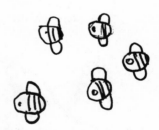

Busy Bees, by Katherine Huxtable age 6

73

93   BUTTERFLY

I wish I was a butterfly
As blue as the sky.
I'd go so high.
By and by
I'd reach the sky
And on a cloud I'd lie.

Patricia Wright

94   IN THE SUMMER

In the summer old birds teach
Their little ones the way to screech.

Nancy Davies

95   SEAGULLS

The seagulls are such funny birds
They hover in the sky.
They fly and scream above the sea
They twist about the sky.

Patricia Wright

Seagulls, by Graham Sanderson age 6

RED ROOSTER

Red rooster in your grey coop,
O stately creature with tail-feathers
                red and blue,
Yellow and black,
You have a comb gay as a parade
On your head:
You have pearl trinkets
On your feet:
The short feathers smooth along your
                back
Are the dark colour of wet rocks,
Or the rippled green of ships
When I look at their sides through
                water.
I don't know how you happened to be
                made
So proud, so foolish,
Wearing your coat of many colours,
Shouting all day long your crooked
                words,
Loud . . . sharp . . . not beautiful!
                        Hilda Conkling

LARK

Lark!
Little black speck
Jumping up invisible steps
Into the sky.
Tweet, twoo!
Tweet, tweet, twoo!
Singing your tweetery song.
Then diving down into the field.
Quiet.
                        Gillian Hughes

98   **THE LOST ARMY**

I lost my army in a great war
Down by the stream I lost them.
Now I doubt as I look through the
              water
If I shall ever find them.

                   Jimmy O'Shea

99   **ITCH**

It was just a queer itch;
A tickle;
A very queer tickle;
Two tickles on top of each other;
A mosquito bite.

                   Gillian Hughes

100   **INFLUENZA**

You're most better
When you've got it.
But when you're getting better
You're worse.

                   Gillian Hughes

101   **FIRST POEM**

Like silvery echoes,
Newly sounding,
In the midst of golden sun.
Crowned with glory angels telling,
All is done.

                   Helen Foley

Once upon a night of stars
One saw a little girl looking up at it.
'Don't look at me so hard, little girl.
How I wonder what you are, too.'
                    Dorothy Jones

The Star, by Rachel Dewick age 6

SEVEN YEARS

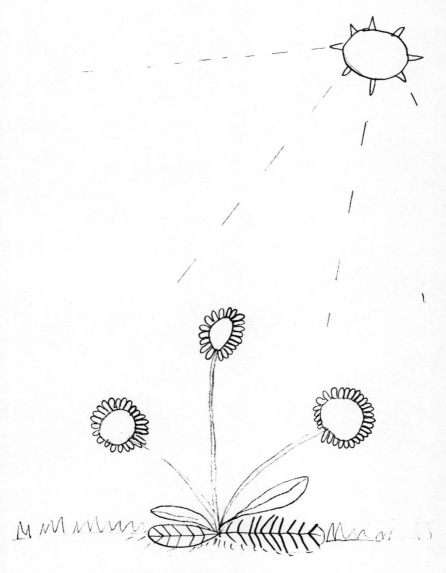

A Daisy, by Arabella Bate age 7

HOW I WRITE A POEM

I think instead of putting down just
any old kind of word that
comes into my head.
Instead I think I should put a different
word that means the same
thing only I think the word
should sound better in my
poem.
That is the way I write my poem.
I think that other people should make
their poem that way and
describe it.
Water rises from a fountain
Gloomy clouds slowly cover the air
With dark black masses of raindrops.

Edward Hogg

GOING TO SCHOOL

I put on my hat and coat and out of
the gate I go.
If it's cold and windy outside I skip
and run to get warm.
But if it's a warm day I sort of think
about things and drag
behind.
My mother says hurry up hurry up!
But I just can't because I'm thinking;

Christopher Guard

105   EXPLANATION ON COMING HOME
LATE

We went down to the river's brink
To of those clear waters drink,
Where the fishes, gold and red,
Ever quickly past us sped.

And the pebbles, red and blue,
Which we saw the green weeds
            through
At the bottom shining lay:
It was their shining made us stay.
                   Richard Hughes

106   ALL ABOUT GOD'S WORK

First there comes the cool green grass,
Then there comes the animals that
            pass,
Then come the tree trunks that belong
            to the trees,
Then come the dancing leaves,
            blowing in the breeze,
Then comes a space where nothing
            much goes,
Then come the birds, who swoop like
            water flows,
Then come the clouds sailing by,
Then comes a space and then the sky.

But, above all, is God on high,
The ruler of all that passes by.
                   Jill Goulder

107   THE STARS

I looked out of the window
And saw a great star shining.
I looked again and saw some more
All shining in the dark.
I looked again and saw the moon
As round as round could be
And all the time I was looking,
The night was going on.

Christine Adams

108   FOSSILS

When I hold a fossil
In my hand
It's like holding
A world of history.

Jackie Shumaker

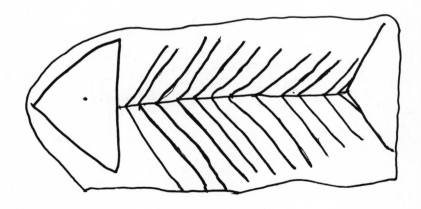

Fossils, by Joanna Kerry age 7

109   IDEAS

Have faith in yourself.
Your Ideas live for ever.
Others will build on your Ideas.
They will grow for ever.
If you think you're a nothing
You've made a big mistake.
Everyone is needed.
As I've said before
Ideas big or small
Grow.
The littlest Ideas
Can grow to be the biggest.
Your Ideas are needed
To build the world.
Because of this people become famous
And the world becomes
A better world than before.

                              Steve Garris

110   WAVES

Have you noticed things that I have
About the waves?
Like armies chasing you.
As you turn, they slowly shrink;
The oysters fall in gathered heaps
Upon the sand.
That's what I notice, do you?

                              Edwin Foot

111   SEA

Sweet corals clinging to the rocks
And mermaids smelling sweet pink
          flowers,
Little turtles on the rocks,
Fishes swimming swiftly past.
There grows seaweed almost like
          bushes,
Singing seaweed dancing against the
          tide.
                          Anne Malindine

112   THE WIND AND THE CHILD

'Tell me, big Wind,
Why are you blowing?
Tell me, big Wind,
Where are you going?'

'Who-oo!' said the Wind,
'I am off to the sea
Where white-capped waves
Are dancing with glee!'
                          Ann Farrer

113   WHEN EVERYTHING WAS STILL

When everything was quietly quiet
When everything was still,
There came a tap-tap-tapping at the
          door.
I thought it was an elf,
But when I opened the door
There was nothing there but leaves.
Yet there was no wind to blow them
          there.
                          Grace Garratt

114 THE WIND

The wind is howling round the house
So baby cannot sleep.
But then it all goes quiet again
As quiet as a mouse can creep.
So now little baby you can slumber
              deep deep deep.
                                    Patricia Pierce

115 THE BABY'S BED

Under covers in a small bed
There are small eyes and a little head;
All night long they sleep in this bed,
These little eyes and little head.
Blue are those eyes,
As blue as the skies;
It's a little round head
In that tiny bed.
                                    Jacqueline Pointer

116 SOUNDS

I like the sounds of wind
As it brushes against the
Chestnut trees
It seems to have
A sweet song that I
Sing to my baby brother.
                                    Laura Harlan

117   MELODY

I'll sing you a melody
Mela mela meloly,
I'll sing you a song.
And I'll sing you a hymn,
Hyma hyma hymnaby.
If you say it's nice,
I'll sing you everything.

                  John Pankhurst

118   THE LAKE

The lake is still.
Nothing breaks the silence.
Deep blue waves swirl around
And creamy white lily pads float.
Pure white ducks paddle around
In the water.
Emerald green frogs splash
In the lake.

                  Ruth Rosenstock

119   OAKU

Oaku with its roaring surf.
Oaku with its tall broad mountains.
Oaku with its blue blue sky.
Oaku with its swaying palm trees.
Oaku with its shining sun.

                  Robin Williams

120   SUMMER TIME

When I first went out to play
I just could not bear to look,
The sun was far too hot.

Under the sun and under the trees,
Oh what a lovely feeling!
I wish I often went outside
Underneath the velvet blue sky.
                              Anne Malindine

121   TO SUMMER

The summer is bright,
And the evenings are light,
And the lark sings high up in the air.
The summer has come,
With its beautiful sun,
And the people may now have a pear.
                              Edith de Wilde

Summer, by Kin Yee Kan age 6

122   SUMMER

Summer has come
The hot wind blows
The farmer sings as he goes
The cattle are out
There are squirrels about.
                        Wendy Hancock

123   WINTER

Animals are shut in
Birds have gone away
But all the little foxes
Have come out to play.

The frost has come, the snow and ice
Covers the farmyard with a sheet of
                white.

Squirrels, dormice, hedgehogs,
                fieldmice
All are fast asleep
All round by the old oak tree
With all those leaves in a heap.
                        Wendy Hancock

THE BUNNY

I saw a bunny
He was ever so funny
He had a white knob
Which went bibbety bob.

He had two long ears
And two pink eyes
Four little legs
And a little black nose.

Shirley Fleet

A Bunny, by Lucy Churall age 7

125 LITTLE TOTS

I had a little kitten
And she was white as snow
But she died soon afterwards
And I was left so lonely.

Her ways were so frolicsome
There is no mistake
But kittie got sumptive
And so she died.

LITTLE TOTS

She sat in her basket
And dozed all the day
And I dressed her in doll clothes
Which made her quite pretty.

She was the dearest kitten
That I ever had
She was always so merry
And so was I too.

I told you she was snowy
But she got dirty soon after
And I was so sorry
I could play with her no more.

I must have another
In place of poor tots
It is most disheartening
For her to die.

May Tait

126   TO ROBIN

Dear little robin,
Where is your nest?
I cannot see it
Wherever may be it,
Because you know best.

Melissa Dring

127   DON'T FLY AWAY

Please little birds, don't fly away.
We want you to stay.
When you sing
The world does ring
With the merry sound of children
          laughing.

When you sit on the telegraph wires
We know that summer is gone
And that you will leave us alone in the
          wintry days
But dear little Robin stays.

                    Jennifer Elmore

128   POOR BIRD

Little bird flew away
One very windy day.
He fell upon a stack of hay,
And there in aching pain he lay.

Little boy found that bird
One horrid stormy day.
His little heart was deeply stirred,
He made it glad enough to stay.

When it got better it lived in trees
          nearby.

                    Brian Herbert

129   THE TREE CREEPER

The wee bird
Creeping up the tree
Never even heard
Or saw me.

                    Alison Britton

THE BLACKBIRD

I saw a blackbird, yes, I'm sure,
Sitting in the hawthorn tree,
It blinked and snapped its yellow beak,
And sat and stared at me.
Pretty bird, come down to me,
Do not be afraid,
I have crumbs awaiting you,
And not a cruel cage.

Doreen Moore

A Blackbird, by James Winter age 7

131   I'D LOVE TO BE A LITTLE LEAF

I'd love to be a little leaf
Upon a tree so high,
I'd whisper to the bumble-bees
As they go buzzing by.

Margaret Drury

IF I HAD SILVERY WINGS

If I had silvery wings
I would do such wonderful things.
I'd fly to the lands above
And fly like a pretty white dove.
I would go so high in the summery
                    breeze
And talk to the rustles
Of old oak trees.

                              Patricia Wright

I WISH I WAS A FISH

I wish I wish I wish
I wish I was a fish
But then the people might catch me,
And put me on a dish.
Then I would be a shark
That weighed a million tons
Then I would marry and have many
                    sons.

                              Hilary Shaw

A Fish, by Christopher Hemming age 7

THE DAISY

I have a little daisy
Its petals diamonds are,
Beneath is ruby red,
Its stalk is emerald green.
Alas the people just walk past
As if my little daisy
They'd never, never seen.
But my little daisy does
What it is told
And my little daisy has
A heart of pure gold.

Patricia Pierce

The Daisy, by Elizabeth Williams age 7

135   CHRYSANTHEMUMS

Chrysanthemums are sometimes
            copper, sometimes red.
Their green leaves are finger-shaped.
Their flowers are round.
They smell of dewy grass.

                                    Leslie

136   THE LITTLE DROP OF RAIN

I saw a little tiny drop of rain
And I said, 'Will you come and see me
            again?'
He said, 'Oh I will, Oh I will, Oh I will.'
And next day I saw him on the
            window sill.

                              Patricia Pierce

137   THE SUNBEAM

I got a little sunbeam
And put it in my pocket,
So when the dark came
I had still got it.

                              Julian Levay

138   THE NEEDLE

Going in and out the cloth
Not with just one tiny stop.
On and on the needle goes
On and on the needle goes.

                              Clare Wright

96

THE LOOM

Click clack bang
Goes the loom.
There is no silence
In the room.
In and out
The shuttle goes.
Click clack bang.

Clare Wright

EIGHT YEARS

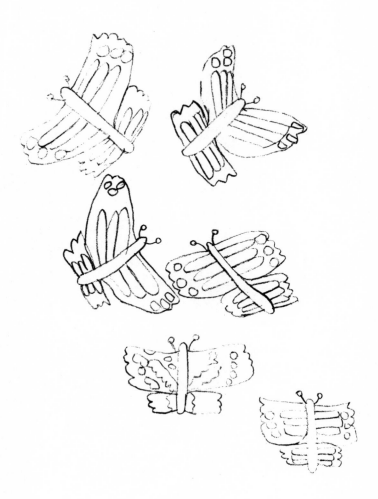

Butterflies, by Sophie Houdret age 8

140   THE COMING OF THE POEM

A poem has got to be born.
It cannot come out when you want it
        to;
It must be born.
When you want to make a poem you
        cannot make it,
But when you do not want to make it,
        it comes.

                  Gillian Hughes

141   WHAT IS A POEM?

When I want to write a poem about
        snow
I think — how does it fall?
And why do we play in it?
I think hard and hard.
Every time I think hard and harder.

I get the Idea
I get to understand it
I feel it in my heart.
That is how I make the snow come
        true.

                  Haitma Ahmid

142   A FREE LIFE

Reading is like a different world
Completely, a secret cage.
No one ever knows what is concealed
        in my mind.

A FREE LIFE

A free life is like flying.
A magic wind gently lifts your heart
Like a pair of wings that let you glide
in freedom.

In my land it is a land of the future
A world of a dream,
What is in your world?

Oh when the water turns green
Like a mirror, it shows the fruit of the
earth,
The spirit of God
And the excitement of the future.
(You can't get these ideas without the
green water.)
Hope Elliot

143   THOUGHTS

My thoughts keep going far away
Into another country under a
different sky:
My thoughts are sea-foam and sand;
They are apple-petals fluttering.
Hilda Conkling

144   MUSIC

Music is like sparkling water,
Like the sea we are to cross.
With adventures before me
I dream of the land to come.
Hope Elliot

145   FOUNTAINS

I do not like dead fountains.
They should be living things
With musical, soft voices.

Grace Garratt

146   THE FOUNTAIN

The fountain squirts
Up up into the
Shiny night like
Old Faithful
When it blows its top.

Billy Kennedy

147   THE FOUNTAIN

The fountain spouts in the air
The silver water
Springs down
Into the husky trees.

Maurine Zahner

148   THE FOUNTAIN

The fountain flutters
Twists and winds
And dribbles down again.

149   THE FOUNTAIN

Cool water rising
Into the warm air
Flying like smoke
From a brown pipe.

David

150   THE HARPER

Up in the clouds
Way far up
A harper is playing
A harp.
The tone of flashing
Music jumps to
Cloud to cloud.
Dash down to earth,
But do not strike
The ground.
You're too beautiful to die,
But splash
Your precious music
Everywhere.

Hope Elliot

151   CLOUDS

White clouds come up.
They are the ships of the sky.
They spread snowy sails
And float far far away.

Grace Garratt

THE MOON'S PATHWAY

Moon, moon shine a pathway in the
        sea
And do not stand behind the poplar
        tree
That stands upon the rugged cliff.
When the wind gives a whiff
Do not hide your face with your veil
But gently sail.

Moon do shine a pathway in the sea
So the spirits of the waves may tread
Where they can see.
'Yes, my child, I will make a pathway
        in the sea
Thank you for reminding me.'
                Patricia Wright

153   THE SUN

The sun breaks over the earth
Like a golden carpet spread.
                Grace Garratt

154   THE RAIN

The rain
Storms
Swishes
Wishes
Whistles
Slishes.
It comes down
On my big brown roof.
It sounds like a thunder bird
Tramping on it.
                Susy Theme

AFTER THE STORM

The storm is over and gone away,
Not a bird sings, not a twig moves.
There's driftwood on the beach and
      the sea is low,
After the storm
After the storm.

But there *was* a sound,
Was it a rabbit scurrying
Or a dog barking?

No, no, no,
It was the whisper of the trees
Far away,
Far away.

                Wendy Hancock

156   THE SEA

The sea is coming, coming, coming,
Pushing the pebbles down the beach;
The caves are green the rocks are grey,
The sand is pulling, pulling, pulling,
Down under the corally sea.
The shells are crackling and breaking
      down the beach,
The beach is silent but for the rushing
      waves.

                Wendy Hancock

157   THE BREEZE

I like to hear the rush of sparkling
                waterfalls
Roar from the top of gold hills,
Mixed with the cool breeze of winter.

I like to feel the breeze
That's the same as the breeze from the
                cool fresh water of the
                        ocean.
                                Ruth Rosenstock

158   THE RIVER

The peaceful river
Glides along
In her beautiful soft green gown.
                                Grace Garratt

159   THE STREAM

I love to see the stream
Upon a summer's day.
I like to see it sparkling
With the river running,
The trout with different colours
That shine beneath the sky.
                                Christine Bridges

The Fish, by Stephen Fisher age 7

160   THE FISH

Swish swish
There goes the fish
As he darts through the seaweed and
        slime
It's slimy and grimy beneath the white
        foam
Especially in a fish's home.
                  Wendy Hancock

161   LITTLE SNAIL

I saw a little snail
Come down the garden walk.
He wagged his head this way . . . that
        way . . .
Like a clown in a circus.
He looked from side to side
As though he were from a different
        country.
I have always said he carries his house
        on his back . . . .
To-day in the rain
I saw that it was his umbrella!
                  Hilda Conkling

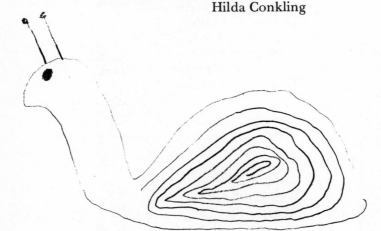

Little Snail, by Nicola Cooper age 8

THE BEE

I am a bee,
A busy, busy bee
I make my honey
So sweet and lovely.
I feed my baby,
So good and funny.

Sylvia Hill

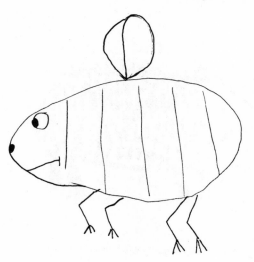

The Bee, by Frances Davidson age 6

163   BEES

The bumble bees they buzz around
In fluffy coats of down;
The Queen is in the hive, so fine
Wearing a velvet gown.

The worker bees are in the bells,
Then in the cups they dive;
The drones are singing lazily,
Then sleep within the hive.

Lalage Prime

164 THE HEDGEHOG

In the corner of the greenhouse,
His prickles quivering in the wind.
Talks quietly to a spider now and
        again,
But to the gardener's heavy boots
He is blind.

                Eleanor Frost

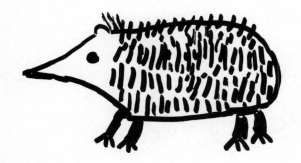

The Hedgehog, by Georgina Pelham age 8

165 CATS' SONG

Up there on the roof tops
Sit the cats yowling
Screaming and howling
And singing such wonderful songs
Topsy and Timmy are singing with
        Jimmy
Tingy and Leppy are singing together
Goldy and Silver chorus with Dover
While Domino sings by herself.

             Wendy Hancock

BUTTERFLY

As I walked through my garden
I saw a butterfly light on a flower
His wings were pink and purple
He spoke a small word . . .
It was *Follow*!
'*I cannot follow*'
I told him,
'*I have to go the opposite way.*'

Hilda Conkling

A Butterfly, by Carla Pitt age 8

167 THE SWAN

The swan comes gliding down the river,
Her black eyes like buttons,
Her white fluffy feathers flapping
                gracefully,
Her beautiful red beak ruffling the
                water.
Her feet paddle behind her,
As the water ripples past,
Her neck swoops down like an arch of
                snow,
And her reflection follows.

Jill

168 THE BLACKBIRD

The blackbird's beak is golden yellow
His feathers are shiny black,
He sings such happy little tunes
I'd love to sing them back.

169 OWL

A wise old owl
With wicked green eyes
Flashes through the night.
A tiny mouse
Dives into his darkened hole.
He dashes past
The gloomy shadows.
The whistle of the wind
Groans
And scatters about.

Darcy Lenz

An Owl, by Helaina Alexandrou age 8

170   TODAY

Damp shaggy lazy
The dull trees are droopy,
They are no longer thought of.
No more does their beauty
Swing past us.

Lynn Rondon

171   THE WOOD

I love the wood
Because it is so dark.
The tall trees
Thick in summer,
But in the winter bare.
The snowdrops glisten in the snow,
The wild roses in the spring,
The bluebells in the summer,
And blades of grass so thick.
In autumn when the leaves fall down,
We go shuffling in them.

Julia Hill

172   IN THE FALL

In the fall the leaves turn brown,
And with the wind they come
            tumbling down.
When I see them on the grass,
I begin to work and rake them fast.
When I get them into a pile
I watch the window for my mother's
            smile.

Charles Hooper

173   SNOW

Snow falls down from the sky
Like leaves, it floats this way and that.

174   THE THUNDER

The thunder is tremendous
Shooting across the sky
With desperate thoughts in its mind
As the rain still goes on
The clouds close in on the earth.
                         John D'Addona

175   THE WIND

The wind is slashing the earth
Like he was pushing of its way.
He slices the earth in half
And walks through the cold wet
            dreary night.
                        John D'Addona

THE WHISPERING TREES

The tall straight
Trees whisper in
Their great coats.
Fruit trees whisper
To the rustling wind,
'I am full of blossoms,
Happy that water flows.'
Flowers blossom, sun is out,
Trees wiggle in the breeze.

Richard Correll

177   ## LATE WINTER

Trees still freeze
Waiting for spring to bloom
When their waiting
Has ended
Leaves will dress them.

Rebecca Panzer

178   ## APRIL

April brings blurry showers
Like an iron shield
Dividing us from the sun.
The blue vanishes
Leaving only rejection
Of the devil
And the limp sun.

Hope Elliot

179   OH LITTLE SEED

        Sprout from the ground
        Oh little seed
        You always hide your head
        In the warmth
        Of the silent earth.
        Your wavy leaves
        Must have the beam of gold sun,
        The sprinkle of blue rain,
        But most of all
        Your face of some colour
        Must have
        The secret of the wind.

                              Darcy Lenz

180   LITTLE FLOWER
        OF SILVER

        Sprout from the ground
        Little flower of silver show yourself
        Don't be squashed up in the ground
        Become free on the top of the earth
        Where you can get fresh air.

                        Eduardo Savilagno

181   THE FLOWER

        Down in the forest
        A little flower grew.
        And it grew and it grew
        And nobody knew.

182   LITTLE DAFFODILS

Little daffodils,
How do you grow?
With spades and water
You should grow.
How would you like to be
A rose climbing up a wall?

Roddy Rawlings

183   SPRING IS APPROACHING

Spring is approaching
Flowers open slowly.
Birds flutter in the air
Clouds push each other
Like there's not enough room.
The brown weary grass dies
While the green grass
Springs up.

Jackie Shumaker

184   FLOWERS BLOOM

Flowers bloom in spring.
They seem to spring out
Of the ground
As they come.
The roots look like
Little hands.

Pam Clymer

185   SPRING

I love spring
When flowers come out and birds are
               born:
The little flowers and big ones with all
               their lovely colours,
Red, blue, yellow and mauve,
And when birds fly for the first time —
How they fall over themselves.
I love spring,
When flowers come out and birds are
               born.
                     Janet Hawkins

186   RED SPRING

What are the roses?
The roses are springtime growing
On a green limb.
                     Patricia Grimm

187   SPRING

Red
Red
Red roses
Grow a little taller
So lilies will admire your loveliness.
Also grow faster and tall
So you will be queen
Of *all* roses and flowers.
I care for you
I water you and put plant food
In the black dirt.
At night you bow to me it seems
Thanking me for what I do!

188   BLOSSOMS

I see a blossom.
It blooms
Like a swan
Fluttering in the sky.

Alice Brennan

189   PINK APPLE BLOSSOM

Little apple blossom
Foam over
With the pink of sweetness.
Some day your blossom
Will turn into a red apple
Dancing like a snapdragon . . . .

Darcy Lenz

190   BLOSSOMS OF THE SPRING TIME

I see a little blossom
It is as soft as a bird's feather.
I think that I will snip it
And give it to my mother.
I'll go look for two!

Jill Marsh

191   SUNFLOWERS

Sunflowers, stop growing!
If you touch the sky where those
           clouds are passing
Like tufts of dandelion gone to seed,
The sky will put you out!
You know it is blue like the sea . . .
Maybe it is wet, too!
Your gold faces will be gone for ever
If you brush against that blue
Ever so softly!

                Hilda Conkling

192   DANDELION

O little soldier with the golden
           helmet,
What are you guarding on my lawn?
You with your green gun
And your yellow beard,
Why do you stand so stiff?
There is only the grass to fight!

                Hilda Conkling

193   GOLDEN CORN

Corn slowly rises from the ground
Pushing the earth out of its way
Swaying in the sunlight
Riper than gold
Turned into yellow bread.

                Lynn Rondon

194   LILACS

Glimmering sun
Gleaming with delight,
Glides on our silent lilacs.
Their buds peek out at us
Like creeping foxes.

                              Lynn Rondon

195   MY MOTHER

My mother is the shape of a flower.
She is a flower of mine.
She lives in my heart.
Her arms are leaves about me.

                              Grace Garratt

196   WITHOUT YOU

I'm hardly alive without you,
I can't even speak without you,
I can't even see without you,
Without you
Nothing would be true.

                              Joanna Powell

197   THE UNITED NATIONS

The United Nations
Is like a mother
Who holds all the
World's troubles
In her lap.

                              Kenneth Miller

198   SOUNDS OF THE NIGHT

I listened to all
The wonderful sounds
Of the night.
Coyotes howling
To make you think of spooks.
Sand blowing
Across the desert land.
Indians' feet
Tapping on hard ground.
Pounding of drums.
Horses' feet
Prancing on the ground.
My mother singing
To my baby sister.

Karen Yarnell

199   EVENING

Coyotes howling
Big bright sun behind
The towering mountains
Twilight rising in the pinkest sky.

Austin Inglehart

200   THE STAR

As I looked up I saw a star,
And as it looked down upon me
It seemed to say,
'Come up here, it's like a velvet carpet
of sea.'

Joanna Powell

201   A NEW WORLD

The sun rises slowly
While the moon
Goes down to rest.
It's like a new world to me.

                Steven Adams

202   LAZY JETS

I sit upon my window
Looking into the sky.
I see the little fireflies
Climbing in the sky.
Then they swoop down
Like lazy jets.

                John D'Addona

203   OPENING STARS

I like the pin pin
Of bursting out stars
When they open.

                Betsy Plant

204   NIGHT

Why is night such a mystery?
Such a musical gay shadow of stars?
No one ever trusts night
For night is so mischief
The way it comes and goes so quickly.

                Hope Elliot

FAIRIES

I cannot see fairies.
I dream them.
There is no fairy can hide from me;
I keep on dreaming till I find him:
There you are, Primrose! I see you,
        Black Wing!

                        Hilda Conkling

206   THE MOONLIGHT HORSES

On the roundabout
At the fair
There are beautiful horses
With golden hair.

'Walk up! Walk up!'
Cries the gipsy man;
'Beautiful horses to ride on!
You can!'

They whinny for joy
When the moon does rise
And jump off the roundabout
Flicking the flies.

They trot through the village
As fast as can be,
Round the old farm
Happy and free.

They stop at the farm
To talk to the filly,
Munching the grass
And sniffing a lily.

THE MOONLIGHT HORSES

Then they gallop back home
Up the pebbly lane,
Then up on the roundabout,
Wooden again.

Lalage Prime

207   MY TIPI

The pictures on my tipi
Seem to come alive at night,
But when morning comes
They go to sleep again.

Laura Harlan

208   MY VOICE

I wouldn't make friends with me
I don't like the sound of my voice
And don't say voices don't count
Because they do
My voice lets me down
It sounds like a boy's
I don't want a voice that is squeaky
                and high
Or a voice that is hoarse and low
An ordinary voice
So that I could be
An ordinary person
Do you see?

Cleo Geary

125

209   LUCY

Lucy is a pretty girl
She wanders round and round
She has not got a friend or a pal
Because she's rather dull.

Lynne Cranstone

210   ABOUT A CHILD WHO LIVES AT
THE BACK OF US

I have a little friend
Who's just had her first birthday.
Her name is Susan.
She plays with me
From the back yard.

She is a darling when playing;
She laughs and gurgles too.
She also copies me;
She chews a pair of sun-glasses and a
             powder puff.

Elizabeth Smith

211   THE SEA OF GRASS

Alone in a sea of swaying grass
Nana and I love to pass
We can't swing and sway
Like the grasses on our way
For Nana is too old to play.

Wendy Hancock

212   I KNOW A MAN

I know a man, a funny old man,
He washes his face in a frying pan,
He combs his hair
With a leg of a chair,
He plays ping pong
With a polar bear.

B. Jackson

213   HEAR THE ARABS

Hear the Arabs as they march along
They are shouting ding-a-ling
Happy with their song.

Kathleen Harris

214   THE GYPSIES

The gypsies gay have come to the
               wood
And now when I pass
I see them chit-chatting
And eating all things good.
There's Father's pig and Auntie's hen
Both shut up in a tiny pen.
Both of them ready
For killing and plucking
And eating beside a lovely fire.
The gypsies are ragged
And thieving and poor
And come begging all day at Mum's
               front door.

Alice Barwell

215   MY CLOCK

Is my clock fast?
Or is it slow?
Whatever it is,
I do not know.

                    Laura Ingham

216   WHIZZ BANG

Whizz crack bang
Firework day is here
If only we could have it
Twenty times a year.

                    Doreen Gould

217   LIGHT

Light is the world
Light is something that shines
Light is the stars and the moon
A light is like a white swan
There are red lights, blue, pink, white.
Light is the world.

                    Lynn Rondon

218   FEAR

Fear
Is a strange feeling in the mind
That overtakes faith.

                    Steve Garris

219   TEACH ME

Teach me to grow
Slow o slow
That I
May live not die.

Joanna Powell

220   A HYMN TO GOD

God made our native land so that we
      might be happy.
God made the flowers so sweet and
      the birds that sing to us.
Dear God made everything.
He made the trees that blow in the
      wind.
He made the snow and sun that all
      God's little children might
      be happy.

Judith Patterson

NOTES ON THE POEMS

1 *Bells* According to her father's diary for 1914, Frances Kent, who sent me this couplet, produced it at the age of two years two months.

2 *Ladybirds is Horrid* Lucinda was the third, and apparently the most prolific, of the Broadbent children (see also 31 and 32; Thomas Broadbent 3; Timothy Broadbent 7). The earliest talker, she said this when she was two years seven months. Her mother writes (1963): 'When my eldest son started to talk I started to write down such part of his conversation as amused me, and I have kept a record ever since. The verses are called Songs by their authors, and are delivered in stressed *recitative*, which appears more instinctive than imitative.' Later (1977): 'There were two main periods of verse: one at about two, a delighted repetition of newly learnt poly-syllabic words "Kangaroo, kangaroo" [7], and the other around four, when they would often chant to themselves, in a sort of plain-song, "God is good" [31].' Lucinda won a scholarship to Wadham College, Oxford, and went up in Michaelmas 1977 to read Politics, Philosophy and Economics.

3 *Bu'fly* Thomas Broadbent (see above note) was two years five months when he said this.

4 *Starlings* See also 57. 'Said several times in a matter-of-fact voice' (mother: January 1963) at the age of two years nine months by a great-great-great-grandniece of R. D. Blackmore.

5 *Snowman* Composed at the age of two years four months. Ben Howison's father notes (January 1963): 'This was produced quite spontaneously, and came out all at once, with scarcely a pause. I wrote it down immediately, and have since made no alterations at all.' The poet phoned his permission to print the poem from Oakham School, where he is currently (1977-8) taking his A levels.

6 *Mr Dye* Composed at the age of two years eight months. The last line was not part of the original poem, but was added some weeks later. Christopher Parish writes (December 1977): 'I can't remember many of the circumstances connected with its composition except that Mr Dye was a sort of rag doll made of two dusters, a check pattern one forming the face and a plain one the body. He didn't, strangely, sport a tie!' He has not written poetry since, and his only publications have been 'a few articles in a numismatic journal of very limited circulation'.

7 *A Sort of Giraffe* Timothy Broadbent (see note on 2) writes (December 1977): 'I got two honorary mentions in the *Daily Mirror* Children's Literary Competition, but never alas a prize; the closest I came to fame was when I made a couple of records with David Bowie ("Moonage Day Dream" and "Hang on to Yourself"). The only work of any merit I've done is my thesis for a Master's degree in Philosophy.'

8 *Lullaby* Peter Simpson's father writes (April 1961): 'We were at tea one afternoon, and our little girl of about one and a half was lying in an armchair, a little fractious. So I asked her brother, of about three and a half, to go over and quiet her. As he bent over the arm of her chair, I heard him half-chant [the two lines]. Where he got the imagery from I have not the least idea.' Cf. the following conversation recorded by Pamela Glenconner:

'One night, do you know, Mummy, I saw Japan.'
'And what was it like?
'Oh, dear little men, dressed all in red, golden giraffes, and gardens of shells.'

(*The Sayings of the Children.*)

9 *On Bodmin Moor* Patrick Buxton's mother writes (January 1963): 'We first came to Cornwall when Patrick was three and a half. It was getting dark as we drove across Bodmin Moor, and the moon was coming up through a lot of cloud, and glinted now and then on bog pools. Patrick was quiet in the back seat, and we thought he was asleep, when he suddenly said this in a funny sing-song little voice. It fitted the loneliness and desolation and general queerness of Bodmin Moor in that stormy light so well that I have never forgotten it. I might add that we had been driving for some hours and hadn't spoken at all for some time before, so Patrick was not rephrasing anything my husband and I had been saying.' Patrick Buxton, who remembers nothing of the circumstances, says (January 1978) that he has 'written nothing of any merit since'. He is training to be a mathematics teacher.

10 *A Rainbow* See also 67, 68, 70, 71, 73, 75, 78, 79, 80, 81, 82, 84, 85, 86, 92, 97, 99, 100, 140. Gillian Hughes was born in Cambridge in 1937, and moved to Stratford-on-Avon in 1939. This is the earliest of 120 poems she sent me in December 1951. She wrote then: 'My parents, although they were very interested in my poetry, never considered that it was very extraordinary that I wrote it. It was very rarely a subject for conversation. Most of my poems were written at Stratford-on-Avon . . . . I never had to learn any poetry until I came to Nottingham, where we read it in class and learnt it. Other than nursery rhymes, the only poetry I heard in Stratford-on-Avon was from Shakespeare's plays which I heard at the Memorial Theatre. In my opinion, it was hearing other people's poetry read to me, and having to learn it, that stopped me writing it. I never had the same interest in poetry after that. . . . I dictated much of my poetry to my mother, who wrote it down without making any alterations. Some of my poems were written while I was watching the thing I was describing, but others were written some time after I had had the experience.' She wrote in April 1960: 'Before leaving Stratford-on-Avon I had written 115 poems, most of which were directly concerned with observations of nature or of everyday incidents which had impressed me. After moving to Nottingham my observations were mainly limited to experiences in the garden. . . . At this time I first became conscious

of the influence of school. Homework began to fill my leisure time and I only wrote 18 poems while we lived in Nottingham. Since then I have been engaged in full-time education, which has occupied and shaped my thoughts.' This last letter was written from Homerton College, Cambridge, in her third year of training as a science teacher. The poet, now Mrs Mirrlees, is married to an Oxford Professor of Economics, and is the mother of two daughters.

11 *Ben Ledi* Mrs Florence Thompson writes (January 1963): 'I enclose three poems produced by my daughter over the past two months. She will be four in April.'

12 *Bonning About* The poet, my goddaughter, will shortly be qualified as a doctor. 'Thinking back I can remember only its repetition in connexion with some Danish posters in our Wells attic, and thinking that the bonning went on in mid-air over Waterlow Park.' She has sent me the music to which she sang it.

13 *The Princess* 'My younger daughter, Anna, who is aged three and a quarter, often chants "poems" of a sort, and when I have time I write them down' (mother's note: April 1963). Anna Machin herself writes (December 1977): 'I can't remember what prompted "The Princess", but I do know that I used to talk and sing to myself almost continually, and that if my mother could find a wobbly crayon, a scrap of paper and the time, she would scribble down my chants. . . . I do not write much now although I am studying English at A level, together with Art and Sociology. I think that my creativity has been directed more towards painting and sculpture and cookery than to poetry.'

14 *Silver Polar Bears* This is all that her mother 'could remember and write down of a "bath song" Roberta produced when nearly four' (mother's note: April 1961). Roberta Nesham herself has since written (December 1977) that she has 'abandoned the arts for more mercenary science': she is an actuary. Her mother is a writer, and two books of fairy stories have been published under her maiden name, Félicité Berryman.

15 *The Butterflies' Song* 'Sung at the piano by a child aged three years and six months': note in *Fifty New Poems for Children*.

16 *The Robin* See also 60. A section of twenty-seven lines has been omitted after the line 'There's notes and notes and notes'. Hugh Bradford's mother writes (June 1961): 'I couldn't always keep pace with him after he started off. The poem occupied his mind for days on end, and he could remember the earlier parts as he went on. They were delivered with much expression and emphasis and drawing out and condensing of different words. "Landscape" is in household use as I am a painter. "There are notes and notes and notes" refers to my hurried scribbles of what he was saying.'

17 *The Lollipop* Garnet Frost (see also 46) is brother of Eleanor (164).

18 *The Brook Dance* See also 22, 40, 41, 49, 96, 143, 161, 166,

191, 192, 205. Hilda Conkling's mother, Grace Hazard Conkling, was Professor of English at Smith College, Northampton, Massachussets, and was herself a musician and poet. When I first heard from Miss Conkling (February 1963), she was working full-time in the bookstore of Smith College, and hoping 'to get myself back in print one way or another'. In her most recent letter to me (December 1977) she writes: 'Now, at an advanced age, I look back at the poems in both books [*Poems by a Little Girl* and *Shoes of the Wind*] with wonder! I have gone on writing, off and on, but having to make a living mostly off. I have enough for a new book but have done nothing about it as yet. Also my autobiography eventually. Sold poems to the *Ladies' Home Journal*, *Christian Science Monitor*, and others. Also made a record of reading my poems for Caedmon Records, New York. One way to preserve them, I thought, as the books are out of print.' See also Introduction.

19 *The Wonderful Singer* Written on Christmas Day 1920, and sent me by Nancy Davies, now Mrs Taylor, with other poems (26, 61, 94) c. 1960. She has written to me since (January 1977): 'These verses "happened" to me when I was four years old. My mother told me later that I would say, "Quick — it's coming", and I would say the verse without conscious thought. . . . "Snowflakes" [61] must have been written after my first remembered sight of snow; and "The Wonderful Singer" happened on Christmas Day while watching my mother's help sweep up the kitchen floor. This unconscious creativity happens to my elder granddaughter. While watching television I have heard her *sing* verses to a remarkably true folk-type tune — four rhyming verses at a stretch — and quite unrelated to the programme she was watching.'

21 *O Happy Hours* The poem was sent me by Mrs E. F. W. Neale, sister of Charles Wintringham who was killed in a RAF accident before the Second World War. It had been written out by its young author, even with the exclamation mark.

22 *To a Flower* See note on 18.

23 *Night* Mary Hemming's grandmother writes (December 1961): 'I overheard her making rhymes after she had been put to bed at night. It was winter, and her room was dark except for a light from the landing.'

24 *The Sea* 'I submit two or three lines spoken by my son Martin at Felixstowe when he was four. They sparkled immediately and I have always remembered them.' (Letter from his father, January 1963.) Martin Panter himself writes (January 1978): 'The few words I used to describe the waves . . . were spoken while watching the sea at Felixstowe during a family holiday with my aunt who lived there. I can still remember being fascinated by the constant curling and crashing of the waves.' After reading History at Cambridge, Martin Panter spent a year at drama school, and is now a professional actor. 'Now adolescence is past I write very little, and apart from short articles and poems in school and university magazines, I have had nothing published.'

25 *Love* Jane Simon was four and a half when she dictated this to her mother.

26 *The Little Mouse* See note on 19.

27 *Under the Lid* Dorothy Wilson, who sent me the poem, has written later (April 1961): 'I must have had some sense of rhythm even then, for I remember being most insistent in my refusal to change "and far a bigger" to "And a far bigger".' The poem refers to an old desk in which she kept her toys. Her copy is dated 'four years eleven months'.

29 *Satellite* Sent me from America in c. 1960, unfortunately without name.

30 *Poem at Bedtime* 'The following is a spontaneous poem made by my brother at bedtime and said to his father at the age of four or five'. (Sister's note, January 1963.)

31 *God* and 32 *Carol* See note on 2.

33 *Lucy's Carol* Lucy was nearly five years old when, just before Christmas, her mother heard her describing a picture of the Nativity to her doll. 'I'll sing you a song about that', she said, and her mother reached quickly for pen and paper.

35 *Love* See also 65, and his brother Ian's 55. Mrs Gray, herself a writer under her maiden name of Dorothy K. Haynes, writes (April 1961) that her sons' poems were composed before they were able to write: 'They were quite spontaneous, but they sounded so good I made a note of them.'

36 *Monologue* See also 37, 38. 'Spoken out loud to herself and taken down at once *verbatim*'. (Mother's note, January 1963.) Sally de Berker has since written (December 1977): 'I can't really remember what led me to such lofty contemplations at that age. They usually occurred to me after I had been trying to explain the world to my younger brother whom I considered it my duty to educate. I am now a student at Kent University, reading English and American Literature, but the poetry has ceased.'

40 *What is Water?* and 41 *By Lake Champlain* See note on 18.

42 *The Happy Moon* Ian Liston's mother notes (April 1961): 'He was apparently inspired by the excitement of being out after dark on a particularly beautiful, clear night. On reaching home, I asked him to repeat the lines, which he did, and I then noted them down.'

44 *The Violet* Written when five years seven months. 'My daughter, when very young, was a prolific maker of verses. "The Violet" was thought up in a very few minutes one evening when she was waiting for me to turn out her light.' (Mother's note, January 1963.)

45 *Little Bird* Nicola's poem and Barbara's (63) were sent me (May 1961) by Mrs D. Harmsworth, who ran a nursery school in Maidenhead during the Second World War. 'I had children from the age of three until they became seven, and having ideas of my own, not strictly orthodox, experimented in several directions. . . . We had rhythm sessions, when the children sang, exercised or just sat and listened to poetry that I read or recited. Much of this was from R. L. Stevenson's *A Child's Garden of Verses*; and then the

children themselves suggested making their own verses.'

47 *Duck* See also 51, 62. Judith is sister of Rosemary Stinton (see 59). Their mother writes (April 1961): 'Both of them have written verse of a kind from the age of five.' When Judith read an article of mine in which I had quoted some children's poetry, she thought that her own poems were no good at all, 'mostly doggerel'. Her mother also writes: 'When she was at junior school the teachers made too many comments on her poetry, and she turned it out like a sausage machine.' I have since heard, fifteen years later, that Judith Stinton is still writing poetry, and she has kindly sent me *Owl House* (The Black Swan Press, 1976) which is ample evidence that she has survived the phase referred to by her mother.

48 *Duck Legs* This and other poems were sent me by Janet Savage herself at the age of eleven after she had read an interview with me in the *Guardian*. Nearly seventeen years later (December 1977) I have heard again from the poet, now Mrs Lewis. She wrote 'a great deal of poetry in [her] teens and early twenties', and a collection entitled *Poems from 16 to 20* was published by the Oriel Press in 1968.

49 *Mouse* Hilda Conkling (see note on 18) writes (December 1977): ' "Mouse" came about from there being so many in the boarding house basement where my cat caught them.'

50 *Little Mr Buzzly Fly* Valerie Haggie wrote between the ages of five and fourteen; this poem is the first she can remember composing. Like Janet Savage (48), she sent it me after reading the *Guardian* interview in May 1961. Since then (December 1977) she has written: 'All that I can remember of [the poem's] creation is standing in the doorway of our dining-room and watching a fly crawling up and down the diamond-leaded windows. I believe they were steamed up: hence the footmarks.' After reading English at Oxford and doing an education year at Cambridge, the poet, now Mrs Cowley, taught at St Paul's Girls' School, London, and she is at present Head of English at St Helen's School, Northwood. 'I only write poetry very occasionally now: the physical and emotional pressures of teaching seem to drain me.'

51 *A Wish* See note on 47.

53 *The Bonfire* 'Said spontaneously by a little girl just as she was going home full of excitement one November the Fifth.' For sending me this poem and Judith Patterson's (220) in February 1961, and for her comments, I am indebted to their former teacher, Miss K. M. Tomlinson.

55 *The Christmas Tree* Ian Gray's mother writes (April 1961): 'He sang the song to himself, quite coherently, and then subsided into gibberish.' See also note on 35.

56 *Christmas* Quentin Neill writes (December 1977): 'I do vaguely remember writing a poem about the moon which won a prize in our local parish magazine, but had no idea that my work had been read by anyone outside the cosy atmosphere of my childhood environment. I do not write poetry any more but dabble in paint-

ing and illustrating' — of which he sent me a fascinating sample.

57 *School* See note on 4.

58 *Cold* See also 91.

59 *The Wind* By the sister of Judith Stinton: see note on 47. Rosemary Stinton, now a professional librarian, is currently (1977-8) working for a Master's degree in Victorian Studies at Leicester University.

60 *Autumn* See also 16.

61 *Snowflakes* See note on 19.

62 *The Clock* See note on 47.

64 *The Singer* 'The muse of poesy descended on my younger son between the ages of four and a half and five and a half, and then deserted him'. (Mother's note, February 1963.)

65 *Happiness* See note on 35. In one of his fine passages of childhood recollection, W. H. Hudson writes: 'The sight of a magnificent sunset was sometimes almost more than I could endure and made me wish to hide myself away' (*Far Away and Long Ago*).

66 *The Face* See also 69.

67 *Dressing Up and Pretending* For this and subsequent poems by Gillian Hughes, see note on 10.

72 *Dandelion* See also 133. Hilary Shaw, who graduated in English at Leicester University and now teaches English as a foreign language in Florence, writes (February 1978): 'I wrote a great many poems as a child, and I sometimes woke up remembering the words having dreamt them. . . . I stopped writing poetry entirely at the age of fourteen or fifteen.' She writes short stories but has not published any.

74 *Aunt Jean* Addressed to a 'charming newly acquired young aunt-by-marriage'.

83 *Lombardy Poplar* Dictated by Crispin Pickles at the age of six and three-quarters to his mother, who sent it to me in October 1961. He had been 'very much influenced by the rhymes in George Macdonald's *At the Beck of the North Wind* which was being read to him at the time'. He has since written (March 1978): 'I do not now write but think that I teach others to do so.'

87 *Rain* See also 90, 138, 139. Clare Wright, daughter of the sculptor Austin Wright, is now a 'cellist with the Bournemouth Symphony Orchestra.

88 *Trees and Clouds* Roger Cohen writes (December 1977): 'I still write but have yet to publish.' He has in fact published articles in *The Paris Metro*, an English magazine based in Paris, where he teaches English and English Literature to private pupils.

89 *Pond at Evening* Paul Dehn notes: 'You'll observe, of course, that where Shakespeare dared only to use the word "howl" four times in a single line in *King Lear*, our six-year-old poet has used it five times and, what's more, got away with it. "Bobby-nut" is an exquisite blend of:

      (a) The *derivative*. Adults had made familiar the name "Bobby" and the word "nut".

NOTES ON THE POEMS

(b) The *meaningless*. Juxtaposed, the words are without formal significance.

(c) The *onomatopœic*. It is the kind of word a fish ought to make when bubbling.

I count it as a new and notable addition to our vocabulary of pure sound — even better than that of the fourteenth century poet who:

... took a goose fast by the nek
And made her to say "wheccumqueck".' (*For Love and Money*.)

90 *Fire Fairies* See note on 87.

91 *The Fire* See also 58. Written after Valerie Ormond's father had lit the fire with coke instead of the usual coal.

93 *Butterfly* See also 95, 132, 152. Patricia Wright, now Mrs Dawson, wrote poems from the age of four to twenty. 'As after the age of eight I enjoyed reading poetry, they are bound to have been influenced by what I read', she told me when she sent a number of poems, including some later ones, in c. 1960.

94 *In the Summer* See note on 19. This is the final couplet only of a poem entitled 'Flowers'.

95 *Seagulls* See note on 93.

96 *Red Rooster* Hilda Conkling (see note on 18 and Introduction) writes that this poem owes its origin 'to the fact that the people who owned the house kept Rhode Island Red chickens in their backyard, and I had a pet rooster' (December 1977).

104 *Going to School* This poem was sent me (c. 1960) by Charlotte Mitchell, the actress and poet. Her son, now a professional actor himself (appearing currently in *Filumena* at the Lyric Theatre, London), still writes 'to keep myself sane', and is 'about to embark on a lazy search for a publisher' (December 1977). The final semicolon is copied from the poet's original typescript: I have retained it as it seems significant!

105 *Explanation on Coming Home Late* First published in *Confessio Juvenis* by the author Richard Hughes (*A High Wind in Jamaica, In Hazard*, etc.) who died in 1976.

106 *All About God's Work* Jill Goulder's mother writes (April 1961): 'My daughter finds it terribly difficult to get off to sleep each night, and always asks me for something to think about when I bed her down. One night I suggested she made up a poem about everything she saw outside, and with no further prompting from me, she pondered this and, while lying in bed, made this verse up. Later I got her to write it down.'

108 *Fossils* See also 183.

109 *Ideas* See also 218. It is interesting to compare this poem by a young American with 65 by a young English boy.

111 *Sea* See also 120.

113 *When Everything Was Still* See also 145, 151, 153, 158, 195. Mrs Maysie R. Garratt, also a poet and the mother of Grace, was one of the few to respond to a letter published in the *Christian Science Monitor* in February 1962. She sent me a number of poems which

137

had 'flowed freely from the lips of my daughter at the age of eight years'.

114 *The Wind* See also 134, 136. Patricia Pierce, now Mrs Meadows, continued to write poems until the age of twelve.

115 *The Baby's Bed* The poet, now Mrs Mittelholzer, still writes poems.

116 *Sounds* See also 207.

117 *Melody* John Pankhurst's mother, who sent me this with others of his poems in April 1961, thought that the poems rhymed too much. She attributed this to his reading many poetry books between the ages of six and eight.

118 *The Lake* See also 157.

119 *Oaku* From a school in Hawaii whose name means 'Happy Work'.

120 *Summer Time* See also 111.

121 *To Summer* Published in the 1850s in *The Northampton Mercury* in which other poems by Edith de Wilde appeared.

122 *Summer* See also 123, 155, 156, 160, 165, 211. Wendy Hancock sent me her poems in 1961 when she was eight, and wrote me several letters about them. She has written more recently (December 1977): 'I remember the poems well. I suppose that those which refer to the seasons [122, 123] were inspired by very happy holidays in Devon which contrasted with (what I considered to be) my dull existence in London. Likewise "The Sea" [156] and "The Fish" [160] grew from my very strong affinity with the sea, which again I only indulged for a fortnight each year. I must admit, however, that I was probably influenced by James Reeves whose *Wandering Moon* I used to reread very frequently. . . . The poems were usually written very quickly in (what I considered to be) a flash of inspiration, often between the time my mother started to go upstairs and the time when she reached the top on her way to say goodnight to me.' Wendy Hancock is at present working in Nottingham where she has been researching in the interpretation and editing of Renaissance and Baroque music. She is co-editor of *Chelys*, the journal of the Viola de Gamba Society.

123 *Winter* See above note.

125 *Little Tots* Sent me by May Tait in 1961: 'I am now 86 and my mother saved the original which I still have.'

126 *To Robin* Melissa Dring, now Mrs Little, writes (December 1977): 'I cannot recall the circumstances of writing this poem. . . . I have followed in my father's footsteps, and have become a portrait painter.'

127 *Don't Fly Away* Jennifer Elmore's mother writes (April 1961): 'My husband (who wrote serious books under his own name Ernest Elmore and crime books under "John Bude") and I were always particularly interested in poetry and verse, and read a great deal to Jennifer. She never produced anything very good, only odd little things which she would bring to us and say "this is my new poem". I need hardly say that she was never helped, or that any words were changed: we never criticised her. She went away to school at nine and never wrote any more.'

129 *The Tree Creeper* Quoted by James Britton in his 'Growing Up in Writing' in Boris Ford (ed.), *Young Writers, Young Readers*, with the (fatherly?) comment that the author 'likes nothing better than to be heard *and* seen!' Quoted again by Michael Baldwin in his Introduction to *Poems by Children, 1950-1961*, with the comment: 'Rare indeed is the statement of wonder that is entirely syntactic, and therefore above suspicion'.

132 *If I had Silvery Wings* See note on 93.

133 *I Wish I was a Fish* See also 72.

134 *The Daisy* See also 114, 136.

137 *The Sunbeam* Composed in school, but sent me by Julian Levay's mother.

139 *The Loom* Clare Wright (see note on 87) writes (December 1977): ' "The Loom" was the result of my mother's reading *Silas Marner* aloud to me.'

142 *A Free Life* See also 144, 150, 178, 204. From America.

145 *Fountains* See note on 113.

146 *The Fountain* This poem and the three poems that follow it were written 'to order' at the same time in the same class (see Introduction). Old Faithful is a famous geyser.

156 *The Sea* See note on 122.

157 *The Lake* See also 118.

160 *The Fish* See note on 122.

161 *Little Snail* See note on 18. ' "Snail" — met him in my garden — same with "Butterfly" ' (166). (Letter from Hilda Conkling, December 1977.)

163 *Bees* See also 206 and Introduction. Lalage Prime's mother, the author Honor Prime, sent me several of her daughter's poems in May 1961. 'Lalage was very concerned about rhyme and scansion, and she was told firmly by her teachers what was what. So she didn't experiment as much as she might otherwise have done. She usually wrote her poems in bed in the morning and more often than not she did not change more than the odd word. But sometimes she agonized all day over a rhyme or a weak line. . . . By eleven she had nearly stopped writing.' Honor Prime has written about her daughter's childhood and fantasy world in *Moonface* (Faber & Faber, 1961): 'Helena is not Lalage, but she owes a great deal to her.'

164 *The Hedgehog* Eleanor Frost, now Mrs Gamper, is sister of Garnet (17, 46). She can 'vaguely recall composing "The Hedgehog" ' (December 1977), and believes it was one of her first serious efforts at typing. She continued to write poetry through her teens, and, though she has published nothing herself, now works in the design department of an educational publisher. She has 'some projects under way at the moment: a group of nonsense poems and a couple of children's stories which I keep meaning to do something about.'

165 *Cats' Song* Wendy Hancock (see note on 122) said this of 'Cats' Song' in 1961 when she was eight: 'All the cats I know except

Dover and Jimmy. Tingy stands for Tinkerbell, my own cat, and
Leppy for Leprechaun.' Three weeks later she wrote: 'I am very
sorry I have not written for such a long time. This morning Goldy
had four kittens, one of them white with two black spots, who I
named Dover, and another tabby who I have not named, and two
black twins like Tinkerbell (my cat).'

169 *Owl* See also 179, 189.

170 *Today* See also 193, 194, 217.

171 *The Wood* The teacher, Miss A. G. Lamb, who sent me Julia Hill's
poem and Alice Barwell's (214) in April 1961 said that her pupils
had written them 'entirely for pleasure'.

174 *The Thunder* See also 175, 202.

176 *The Whispering Trees* This is the original version of a poem which
appeared in the *Christian Science Monitor* (10 March 1956) in an
edited form.

180 *Little Flower of Silver* Eduardo Savilagno's first language is Span-
ish.

186 *Red Spring* This poem is written in the Japanese form, *hokku*, the
aim of which is to paint a small picture; to suggest rather than
state; to evoke a mood; to startle by contrast — all in the disci-
plinary compass of seventeen syllables.

195 *My Mother* See note on 113.

196 *Without You* See also 200, 219. 'She wrote them when she was
eight, easily, spontaneously and with few alterations or additions.
Since then she has made few attempts to express herself in this
way.' (Mother's note, January 1963.)

199 *Evening* This poem, like 12, was set to music by its author.

202 *Lazy Jets* See also 174, 175.

206 *The Moonlight Horses* See note on 163. A revised version of this
poem appeared in the *Young Elizabethan*: see Introduction. The
poet, now Mrs Lee, writes (December 1977): 'The poem was
suggested by a trip to the fair that visited Harpenden annually. I
certainly remember being enchanted by the roundabout horses,
as I suppose all children are. . . . I'm afraid my literary efforts
stopped when I was about eleven.'

207 *My Tipi* See also 116. The poet is American. Not every cisatlantic
reader may know that a tipi is the tent-like shelter made by Indians
out of skins, and of course decorated.

208 *My Voice* Cleo Geary won a prize for this poem in the second of
the *Daily Mirror* Children's Literary Competitions.

209 *Lucy* Lynne Cranstone's poem together with poems by B. Jackson
(212), and Doreen Gould (216), were sent me by their former
teacher, Miss M. Belderson, in April 1961. Miss Belderson writes:
'As I am interested in poetry, and try to write a little myself sometimes, I encouraged the children I taught to write — just when they
felt like it, and as you will see they chose their own subjects.
Naturally I did not offer criticism to the children.'

210 *About a Child Who Lives at the Back of Us* Sent me by Elizabeth
Smith's mother in April 1961. In one of her daughter's last poems,

written at the age of ten, a mouse, who lives in a hole and is weak, 'has a little sweak'. Mrs Smith wrote that the 'sweak' was deliberate, not a spelling mistake: it *is* what a mouse says. 'At eleven the poet entered grammar school and found the curriculum hard going: not much time to stand and stare, or to listen for sweakings.' Elizabeth Smith became a primary school teacher.

211 *The Sea of Grass* See note on 122.
220 *A Hymn to God* Sent me by Miss K.M. Tomlinson (see note on 53). 'The poem was written the day after the death of King George VI. The little girl cried when she heard the king was dead, and said, "Who will look after me now?" I told her that she need not feel that she had no one to take care of her as people were really taken care of by God. The following day she gave me the poem, saying, "Please put this to music".'

AFTERWORD AND
ACKNOWLEDGMENTS

To Hilda Conkling and Gillian Hughes I owe my first serious interest in the poetry of childhood. I refer elsewhere to Hilda Conkling, whose *Poems by a Little Girl* and *Shoes of the Wind* are still a source of delight. Gillian Hughes, now Mrs James Mirrlees, was the youngest contributor to John Lehmann's *Penguin New Writing*. Her poem 'Harvest' appeared in number 26 (1945) when she was eight, though it was written when she was six; another poem, 'Calm Sea', appeared in number 30 (1947): I have included neither in this anthology. In 1951 (see note on 10) she sent me 120 of her poems, and we have corresponded to this day, though up to the time of writing we have never met.

At around the time I received Gillian Hughes's poems, I wrote to a number of newspapers in this country and America about my interest. Few of my letters were printed, but those that were produced such a quantity of letters and poems that I had to use most of our housekeeping money on postage. Broadcasts (BBC and CBC), articles and newspaper interviews produced further sackfuls, and in all I must have read literally tens of thousands of poems. By 1963 the anthology, very much as here presented, was ready to publish; and the late Sir Herbert Read, who had given it generous approval, offered to write a Foreword on its acceptance. Unfortunately that was not to be. Many publishers sent encouraging letters, and there seemed to be some very near misses; but the poems have wasted their sweetness in a drawer for many years since then. Their emergence now owes much to Stephen Brook of Routledge & Kegan Paul, and to Charles Causley. I also owe to Sir Herbert my place as a selector for the *Daily Mirror* Children's Literary Competition of whose Advisory Panel he was Chairman. This annual competition, which has done so much for writing in schools, has recently been taken on by W. H. Smith. I must thank another friend and poet, G. S. Fraser, whose sharp criticism of the original Introduction spurred me to revise it. As so often, there has been advantage in delay.

The passage of years has brought another advantage. It is hardly surprising that my efforts to get in touch again with all who sent poems have not been completely successful; but in many cases I have now had the pleasure of corresponding with the poets themselves in addition to the parents or grandparents who formed the first link. Many have expressed both surprise and delight to be reminded of their early poems; and their reflections have added greatly to the interest of the Notes. In every case there has been complete willingness that poems should appear, a fact which has encouraged me to think that those whom I have not been able to trace will not be offended. May I thank them collectively here, and hope still that I may hear from them. I must thank also those many more in number for whom I have not found place in the anthology: not only have they given me pleasure; they have helped in forming views and judgments. It was only at a late stage of editing that I decided to exclude poems by over-eights. There were many which I was sad to lose, but there seemed a marked falling off in quality — perhaps I should say, rather, difference in kind. T. S. Eliot may point a reason for this in that fine short poem 'Animula':

> 'Issues from the hand of God, the simple soul'
> To a flat world of changing lights and noise,
> To light, dark, dry or damp, chilly or warm;
> . . . .

but

> The pain of living, and the drug of dreams
> Curl up the small soul in the window seat
> Behind the Encyclopaedia Britannica.
> . . . .

I have been particularly regretful to have lost touch with a most faithful correspondent from the USA, Josephine Burns Davis. It is thanks to her belief in education as what Eliot has elsewhere called 'a common pursuit of liberation' that some two dozen of the poems appear. To another American lady, Mrs William Klingensmith, I am indebted both for a view of her unpublished thesis on children's poetry and for several poems from her collection.

Although most of the poems appear here for the first time in print, a few have been previously published. For these I make grateful acknowledgment to authors, editors, publishers and copyright holders as follows: Hilda Conkling, *Poems by a Little Girl*, Harrap, 1920 (18, 22, 40, 41, 49, 96, 143, 161,

143

166, 191, 192, 205); Paul Dehn, *For Love and Money*, Max Reinhardt, 1956 (20, 89); lines from 'Animula' in *Collected Poems* 1909-1962 by T. S. Eliot, reprinted by permission of Faber and Faber and of Harcourt Brace Jovanovich, Inc., copyright, 1936, by Harcourt Brace Jovanovich, Inc.; copyright © 1963, 1964 by T. S. Eliot; *Poems by Helen Foley*, Dent, 1938 (101); Boris Ford (ed.), *Young Writers, Young Readers*, Hutchinson, 1960 (129, 167); lines from Kahlil Gibran, *The Prophet*, copyright Alfred A. Knopf Inc. reprinted by permission of Alfred A. Knopf Inc.; Pamela Glenconner, *The Sayings of the Children*, Basil Blackwell, 1918, (66, 69); Richard Hughes, *Confessio Juvenis*, Chatto & Windus, 1926 (105); Siddie Joe Johnson (ed.), *Hokku*, Dallas Public Library, 1960 (186); J.A. Miles (ed.), *Brave Young Singers*, Melbourne University Press, 1938 (112, 128); 'O parrot, thou hast grey feathers' by Louis MacNeice from Louis MacNeice, *Modern Poetry*, © Oxford University Press 1968, reprinted by permission of Oxford University Press; Doreen Moore, *Flashes from the Pan of Youth*, Arthur H. Stockwell (130); Norman Morris, *First Fruits*, Oxford University Press, 1939 (131); *Fifty New Poems for Children*, Basil Blackwell (15); *Poetry and Children*, Methuen, 1956 (52, 54, 168); *And When You Are Young*, Joint Council for Education through Art (58, 91); *Children As Writers* 2, *Daily Mirror* (208); *Home and Family*, 1962 (33); *Parents' Review*, March 1961 (107); *Young Elizabethan*, July 1956 (110, and see note on 206 and Introduction); *The Christian Science Monitor*, 10 March 1956 (154, 176 — see note).

Finally, while I have expressed in the Introduction my first aim in publishing, I must give here a secondary but related one. If other children, parents, grandparents, teachers will send me c/o the publisher further poems, it may one day be possible to produce a successor to this book. I should then have the privilege of sharing once more with readers the experience of Hope Elliot (142) when

> A magic wind gently lifts your heart
> Like a pair of wings that let you glide in
> freedom.

T.R.

INDEX OF POETS

INDEX OF POETS

It has unfortunately been impossible to attach surnames to the
following:

It has unfortunately been impossible to attach any names to the
following poems:

15, 20, 29, 34, 39, 52, 54, 76, 89, 148, 168, 173, 181, 187.

INDEX OF FIRST LINES

149

INDEX OF FIRST LINES

150

9758713 ~~ROGERS~~, T.   Those first
                           affections

-0. AUG. 1986
6/80
       821.008   WS   5.95